THE
SLOW
COOKER

COOKBOOK

THE
SLOW
COOKER
COOKBOOK

GINA STEER

NEW
BURLINGTON
BOOKS

A Quintet Book

This edition printed in 2014 by
New Burlington Books
4th Floor, Sheridan House
114-116 Western Road
Hove BN3 1DD
United Kingdom

ISBN: 978-0-85762-246-4
QTT.SLCC2

This book was conceived, designed and produced by
Quintet Publishing Limited
4th Floor, Sheridan House
114-116 Western Road
Hove BN3 1DD
United Kingdom

Designer: Maria Mokina
Photographer: Jon Whitaker
Food Stylist: Fern Green
Art Director: Michael Charles
Managing Editor: Emma Bastow
Publisher: Mark Searle

Manufactured in China by 1010 Printing International Ltd.

10 9 8 7 6 5 4 3 2 1

CREDITS

We would like to thank Andrew James UK Ltd for supplying the Slow
Cookers for the preparation of all the dishes in this book.
We would also like to thank Russell Hobbs for the use of their
products in the making of this book.

CONTENTS

INTRODUCTION

Once you've gotten used to life with a slow cooker, you cannot imagine life without one. Its versatility is immense, the flavour of the food divine and it is incredibly simple to use. But you probably know this; otherwise, why would you buy this book? However, if your cooker is still sitting in its box in the closet, pull it out, shake off the dust and get cooking!

There are many advantages to using a slow cooker. One of the best is without doubt the way the flavours develop during the long, slow cooking, resulting in an explosion of tastes unimaginable before. The tenderness of the meat is amazing, and this applies to even the cheapest cuts, with the added bonus that all the nutrients of the food cooked in this way are retained. Fish and vegetables, too, take on a completely different taste with none of the flavours lost. Fruit desserts are delicious, chutneys and relishes are full of flavour and ready to eat immediately, no need to leave to mature.

In addition, you do not need to worry that your pot is going to burn dry or that you are using too much fuel. The slow cooker is environmentally friendly, saving up to two-thirds of fuel normally used in a conventional oven. However, there are a few guidelines to bear in mind when first starting to use your cooker.

FOOD PREPARATION

In many of the recipes, the meat or vegetables are seared by frying lightly in a frying pan or saucepan before placing in the cooker. This is to help with the appearance, texture and flavour. However, it is not strictly necessary. If you have very little preparation time, it is possible to skip this step. Likewise, many of the soups have been puréed for a smooth texture and appearance, but again, this is a matter of personal taste.

Frozen foods should be thoroughly thawed before being placed in the cooker, and the cooking time for these is less than for their fresh counterparts. Normally, thawed frozen vegetables or shellfish are added toward the end of the cooking time.

Dried beans should be soaked in cold water overnight or for at least eight hours before cooking in the slow cooker. Some beans, such as kidney beans, must be boiled for 10 minutes in order to kill toxins contained in the bean – check on the package if in doubt. Lentils, however, do not need pre-soaking. With rice, use the quick cooking or converted rice as these are partially cooked and much of the starch has been removed, reducing the risk of the finished rice sticking together. It is always a good idea to rinse the rice before using. Pasta is best added about 40 minutes before the end of the total cooking time. Root vegetables take longer to cook than meat or fish, so it is important that they are cut into smaller pieces than normal and completely covered with the cooking liquid.

A better flavour is achieved with the use of dried rather than fresh herbs during the long, slow cooking process. Fresh herbs can be sprinkled on just before serving to enhance the flavour and appearance of the finished dish.

You can thicken the dish either at the beginning or at the end of the cooking time. Either use flour at the beginning, when searing the meat or vegetables, or stir in cornflour toward the end. You will need to use a little more flour or cornflour than normal if you prefer a thick sauce, because due to the long, slow cooking, the volume of liquid is increased.

COOKER SETTINGS

The slow cooker is controlled by four switches: off, low, high and auto. At the low setting, the cooker will cook at its lowest temperature. When this setting is used, the cooker needs to be preheated on high for 20 minutes. The power light will be on the entire time. With the high setting, the red light will also stay on the entire time and

the cooker will cook at its highest power. If, by the remotest chance the food does dry out, do not simply add cold liquid; switch off, unplug then add warm water. You can then continue cooking.

With the auto cook function, cooking starts at a high temperature, then automatically switches to low cook. The temperature is thermostatically controlled and the light will come on and off. With this facility it is possible to cook during the night, making it possible to cook tomorrow's breakfast or lunch overnight.

Best of all, you can set the cooker before you go to work and come home to a delicious home-cooked meal. Prepare the ingredients the night before and leave them overnight in the fridge (or you can forego searing the meat or vegetables beforehand).

Whichever approach you take, place the empty cooking pot in the slow cooker and place the lid in position. Plug in and switch on, and set the control to high. Preheat for 20 minutes and use this time to bring the cooking liquid to the boil. Once the cooker is heated, remove the lid, add the food to the cooking pot, then pour over the boiling liquid, cover with the lid, and switch the cooker to auto cook. All the recipes give instructions for preheating the cooker. This is important. Your manufacturer's booklet will give instructions for the cooker you have, so do refer to it.

When adapting your own recipes to cook in the slow cooker, simply look for similar recipes in the book and adapt cooking times accordingly.

TYPES OF COOKERS

Slow cookers vary in shape, size and capacity. So when choosing one, there are a few points to bear in mind. All cookers have a low wattage and all consume about the same amount of electricity. The settings vary according to the make and size, so if buying a new cooker, choose one that will meet your needs. Those with an on/off switch have the distinct advantage of preventing the cooker from accidentally switching off during the cooking process.

It is possible to buy an earthenware pot that is permanently fixed into an outer casing normally made of aluminium or heat resistant plastic. Heating elements are placed around the outside of the inner pot between the outer casing and the cooking pot. It is possible to obtain cookers that have a detachable cord to enable the cooker to be taken to the table.

Another type of cooker has a removable inner earthenware cooking pot, which means that only the cooking pot needs to be taken to the table. Food can easily be browned or crisped under the grill using only the cooking pot, thus ensuring the outer casing is not damaged by the heated grill elements. In such cookers, the heating elements are fitted within the outer casing located either on the base or sides.

There are different capacity cookers that vary from 1.5 to 3.5 litres (3 to 8 pints). It is a good idea to buy a large rather than a

small cooker, as it enables you to cook a far greater range of dishes plus cater for more people.

COOKER CARE

Looking after your cooker is simple but very important. Before you use your cooker for the first time, wash in mild soapy water, rinse and dry thoroughly. After use, remove the cooking pot and empty out the food (take care when handling the hot pot; use oven gloves). After emptying, do not immediately plunge into cold or boiling water. Switch off, unplug and fill the cooking pot with warm water. Then wash as before in warm soapy water and rinse well.

If necessary, soak for a few minutes to remove any stubborn pieces of food, then gently brush with a soft brush. Dry thoroughly. Do not leave the cooking pot immersed in water as the porous base could crack when heated. NEVER immerse the outer casing in water; fill with water or use the outer casing for cooking without the inner cooking pot. If the outer casing needs cleaning, wipe clean with a mild detergent, such as dishwashing soap. The lid should also be thoroughly washed, ensuring that the small vent hole is free from any food particles. Do not put any part of the cooker in the dishwasher or use harsh abrasive cleaners, which could damage the finish.

GENERAL TIPS

Check when cooking joints, puddings or foods cooked in dishes such as pudding moulds or gratin dishes that the food or dishes fit comfortably in the cooking pot and that the lid fits securely.

Root vegetables take longer to cook than meat or fish, so cut them up into small bite-size pieces and place in the base of the cooker, completely covering with liquid.

When browning meat it can be a good idea to brown the vegetables as well. Frozen vegetables, fish, shellfish, meat, or poultry should be thawed before using.

Use quick cooking or converted rice and dried pasta, rinsing the rice before use. Add the pasta toward the end of the cooking time. If the cooker has a removable cooking pot, finished dishes can be browned under the grill.

STARTERS AND SAUCES

Sauces are ideal for the slow cooker. The long, slow cooking time brings out the flavours. Starters such as terrines and patés can be steamed on a rack or rivet, and even bread can be cooked in the slow cooker.

RED WINE SAUCE

Remember, the 6 hours refer to the actual cooking time; the extra 2 hours mean that the sauce will hold for a further 2 hours.

MAKES 600 ml (20 fl oz)   **PREPARATION TIME** 15 min   **COOKING TIME** Cook on low 6 to 8 hrs

INGREDIENTS

2 tbsp unsalted butter

4 shallots, peeled and finely chopped

2 garlic cloves, peeled and minced

50 g (1 ¾ oz) mushrooms, wiped and finely chopped

3 tbsp plain flour

300 ml (10 fl oz) red wine

240 ml (8 fl oz) stock

1 tsp redcurrant sauce or clear honey

Salt and freshly ground black pepper

Preheat the cooker on high while preparing ingredients. Heat the butter in a pan and sauté the shallots, garlic and mushrooms for 3 minutes. Sprinkle in the flour and cook, stirring, for 1 minute, then take off the heat. Gradually stir in the red wine and then the stock.

Add the redcurrant sauce or honey and a little seasoning. Return to the heat and cook, stirring. When the mixture comes to the boil, pour into the cooking pot and cover with the lid. Cook on low for 6 to 8 hours, adjust seasoning, and either serve as it is or strain, then serve.

POTATO SOUP WITH CORIANDER

If preferred, this soup could be served slightly chunky. Instead of passing through a food processor, simply mash the cooked ingredients with a potato masher.

SERVES 4   **PREPARATION TIME** 25 min   **COOKING TIME** Cook on low 5 to 6 hrs   **AUTO COOK** 6 to 9 hrs

INGREDIENTS

25 g (1 oz) unsalted butter

4 shallots, peeled and chopped

2–3 garlic cloves, peeled and chopped

450 g (1 lb) potatoes, peeled and chopped

2 carrots, peeled and chopped

1 small apple, peeled, cored, and chopped

Grated zest and juice of 1 unwaxed lemon

1 tsp ground cumin

1 tsp ground coriander

Few strands of saffron

1 tbsp plain flour

750 ml (25 fl oz) vegetable stock

Salt and freshly ground black pepper

1 tbsp freshly chopped coriander

4 tbsp sour cream

2–4 spring onions, trimmed and finely chopped

Preheat the cooker on high. Melt the butter in a large pan and sauté the shallots, garlic, potatoes, carrots and apple for 5 minutes or until slightly softened.

Add the lemon zest with the spices, then the flour, and cook, stirring, for 2 minutes. Remove from the heat and gradually stir in the stock followed by the lemon juice. Add a little seasoning, then return to the heat and bring to the boil. Spoon or pour into the cooking pot and cover with the lid.

Reduce the temperature to low and cook for 5 to 6 hours. Blend until smooth, then stir in the chopped coriander and adjust the seasoning. Reheat if necessary and serve with the sour cream, and sprinkled with the chopped spring onions.

Left: *Lentil and Squash Broth (page 18)*

SMOKED HADDOCK AND BROAD BEAN CHOWDER

This soup is definitely better if you remove the broad beans from their tough outer skins. It may be a little time-consuming but well worth the effort.

SERVES **4**　　　PREPARATION TIME **25 min**　　　COOKING TIME **Cook on low 5 to 6 hrs**　　　AUTO COOK **6 to 9 hrs**

INGREDIENTS

25 g (1 oz) unsalted butter

1 medium onion, peeled and chopped

350 g (12 oz) new potatoes, scrubbed and diced

1 tbsp flour

475 ml (16 fl oz) vegetable stock

300 g (10 oz) smoked haddock fillet, skinned and diced

150 ml (5 fl oz) semi-skimmed milk

Freshly ground black pepper

75 g (2 ½ oz) sweetcorn, thawed if frozen

100 g (3 ½ oz) broad beans, removed from skins, thawed if frozen

1 tbsp chopped fresh parsley

2–3 tbsp sour cream

Crusty bread, to serve

Preheat the cooker on high. Melt the butter in a pan, then sauté the onion and potatoes for 3 minutes, stirring frequently. Sprinkle in the flour and cook for 2 minutes, then take the pan off the heat. Gradually stir in the stock and bring to the boil. Add the diced smoked haddock. Spoon or pour into the cooking pot, cover and reduce the temperature to low. Cook for 4 hours. Mix the corn and broad beans together then add to the cooking pot and continue to cook for an additional 1 to 2 hours.

Stir in the chopped parsley, adjust the seasoning and serve with spoonfuls of sour cream and chunks of crusty bread.

SUNBURST SOUP

The advantage of cooking soup in the slow cooker is that there is no danger of the soup burning – the flavour just continues to improve.

SERVES **6**   PREPARATION TIME **35 min**   COOKING TIME **Cook on low 6 to 8 hrs**   AUTO COOK **6 to 10 hrs**

INGREDIENTS

3 medium red peppers

1 tbsp oil

1 medium onion, peeled and finely chopped

2–3 garlic cloves, peeled and minced

1 red serrano chile, seeded and chopped

3 ripe plum tomatoes

950 ml (32 fl oz) vegetable or chicken stock

1 tsp soft brown sugar

Salt and freshly ground black pepper

Few sprigs fresh basil

4 tbsp sour cream

Fresh chopped basil, to garnish

Warm Italian bread, to serve

Preheat the cooker on high. Cut the peppers in half, seed and remove membranes, then place under a preheated grill and cook for 10 minutes, turning, or until the skins have charred slightly. Remove from the heat, place in a paper bag and leave for 10 minutes. When cool enough to handle, skin the peppers and slice thin.

Meanwhile, heat the oil in a large pan and sauté the onion, garlic and serrano chile for 5 minutes, stirring frequently. Roughly chop the tomatoes and add to the onions together with the sliced peppers and sauté for 2 minutes. Add the stock with the sugar and seasoning to taste. Bring to the boil, pour into the slow cooker and add a few basil sprigs. Cook on low for 6 to 8 hours. If a smoother soup is preferred, cool slightly, then blend and reheat gently. Swirl with the cream, garnish with the chopped basil and serve accompanied by the bread.

DUCK PÂTÉ

This pâté freezes well and does not change in texture when thawed. It is a great recipe to make regularly and freeze for entertaining.

MAKES **12 slices**   PREPARATION TIME **20 min**   COOKING TIME **Cook on high 4 to 6 hrs**

INGREDIENTS

200 g (7 oz) Parma ham, or prosciutto

675 g (1 ½ lb) duck breast meat

450 g (1 lb) turkey breast meat

100 g (3 ½ oz) bacon

Grated zest and juice of 1 large orange

4 shallots, peeled and finely chopped

1 garlic clove, peeled and minced

Salt and freshly ground black pepper

2 tbsp chopped fresh parsley

¼ tsp fresh grated nutmeg

2 tbsp brandy

2 tbsp orange marmalade

3–4 fresh bay leaves

1 small orange and fresh cherries, to garnish

Preheat the cooker on high. Take a 1.2-litre (2-pint) ovenproof dish that will sit in the top of the cooking pot and line the base and sides with Parma ham, overlapping the sides of the dish. Trim fat from the duck breasts and cut them into very small pieces. Trim the turkey and cut into small cubes. Chop the bacon. Combine the meats in a bowl.

Add the orange zest, juice, shallots, garlic, seasoning, parsley, nutmeg and brandy. Mix well, then spoon into the lined dish, pressing down, and fold the ham over. Cover with aluminium foil.

Place in the cooking pot and pour water around almost to the top. Cook on high for 4 to 6 hours. Remove and cool before turning out. Heat the marmalade and strain. Arrange the bay leaves, orange and cherries on top of the pâté and brush with the marmalade to serve.

LEFT: *SUNBURST SOUP*

MINESTRONE SOUP

Choose your favourite beans for this soup. If using dried beans, soak them overnight or they may be tough. If you opt for tinned beans, drain and rinse, then add to the cooker after sautéing the onions.

| SERVES | **4 to 6** | PREPARATION TIME | **30 min** | COOKING TIME | **Cook on low 6 to 8 hrs** | AUTO COOK | **6 to 10 hrs** |

INGREDIENTS

1 tbsp olive oil

1 medium onion, peeled and chopped

3 garlic cloves, peeled and minced

2 celery sticks, trimmed and diced finely

100 g (3 ½ oz) bacon, chopped

2 medium carrots, peeled and diced

1 large leek, thoroughly washed, trimmed and sliced thin

450 g (1 lb) tin borlotti or haricot beans, drained and rinsed

950 ml (32 fl oz) vegetable stock

2 tbsp tomato purée

Salt and freshly ground black pepper

50 g (1 ¾ oz) uncooked spaghetti

175 g (6 oz) shredded green cabbage

Freshly grated Parmesan cheese and warm chunks of Italian bread, to serve

Preheat the slow cooker on high. Heat the oil in a large pan and sauté the onion, garlic, celery, bacon, carrots and leeks for 5 minutes, stirring frequently. Add the drained beans with the stock and the tomato purée blended with 2 tablespoons of water. Bring to the boil. Pour into the cooker, add seasoning, then cook for 7 hours.

Break the spaghetti into small lengths, add to the slow cooker and continue to cook for another hour, adding the cabbage for the last 30 minutes of cooking time. Check seasoning. Serve with Parmesan cheese and bread.

TOMATO AND BASIL SOUP

The long slow cooking increases the tomato flavour of this soup. Although it is better to use dried herbs, dried basil is not intense in flavour, so add fresh basil toward the end of cooking.

| SERVES | 4 | PREPARATION TIME | 15 min | COOKING TIME | Cook on low 8 to 10 hrs | AUTO COOK | 10 to 12 hrs |

INGREDIENTS

6 sundried tomatoes, chopped

1 tbsp olive oil

1 red onion, peeled and chopped

2-3 garlic cloves, peeled and minced

450 g (1 lb) ripe plum tomatoes, skinned and chopped

1 red pepper, skinned, seeded and chopped

1 tbsp grated orange zest

150 ml (5 fl oz) orange juice

1 tsp sugar

600 ml (20 fl oz) vegetable stock

Salt and freshly ground black pepper

Few basil sprigs

3-4 tbsp sour cream

1 tbsp fresh shredded basil

Shaved fresh Parmesan cheese

1 tbsp cornflour, optional

Warm Italian bread, to serve

Preheat the slow cooker on high. Cover the sundried tomatoes with almost boiling water and let sit for 10 minutes. Then drain, reserving the soaking liquid.

Heat the olive oil in a pan, then gently sauté the sundried tomatoes, onion and garlic for 4 minutes. Add the chopped plum tomatoes with the red pepper and continue to cook, stirring frequently, for 5 minutes. Add the soaking liquid with the grated orange zest, juice, sugar, stock with seasoning to taste, and bring to the boil.

Add the basil sprigs and then pour the soup into the cooking pot. Reduce the temperature to low, cover and cook for 8 to 10 hours. Blend the soup until smooth, adjust seasoning and serve immediately with spoonfuls of sour cream topped with the shredded basil and Parmesan cheese. Alternatively, for a thicker soup, blend the cornflour with 2 tablespoons of water, stir into the soup, and pour into a pan. Cook, stirring, until the soup has thickened slightly, then serve as above with chunks of warm Italian bread.

SWEET POTATO VICHYSSOISE

This soup can be served hot or chilled. If serving cold, it needs to be chilled for at least 4 hours. Garnish just before serving.

| SERVES | 4 to 6 | PREPARATION TIME | 20 min | COOKING TIME | Cook on low 6 to 8 hrs | AUTO COOK | 8 to 10 hrs |

INGREDIENTS

950 ml (32 fl oz) chicken stock

1 medium onion, peeled and finely chopped

2 garlic cloves, peeled and minced

1-2 red jalapeño chiles, seeded and chopped

450 g (1 lb) sweet potatoes, peeled and cut into chunks

1 ripe mango, peeled, stoned and chopped

Salt and freshly ground black pepper

120 ml (4 fl oz) single cream

4 spring onions, trimmed and finely chopped

1 tbsp chopped fresh coriander

Preheat the cooker on high. Place the chicken stock with the onion, garlic, chiles, sweet potatoes and mango in the cooking pot, and season.

Cover with the lid and cook on low for 6 to 8 hours. Cool slightly, purée, then, if serving hot, return either to the cleaned cooking pot or to a clean pan. Stir in the cream, adjust the seasoning, and either heat for 1 hour in the slow cooker, or heat on the hob for 5 to 10 minutes. Stir in the chopped spring onions and coriander to serve. If serving chilled, chill for at least 4 hours, then stir before serving.

LENTIL AND SQUASH BROTH

This soup is ideal to serve when the weather is beginning to turn cold or a bowl of comfort food is required.

SERVES **6**   PREPARATION TIME **25 min**   COOKING TIME **Cook on low 6 to 8 hrs**   AUTO COOK **8 to 10 hrs**

INGREDIENTS

25 g (1 oz) unsalted butter

1 small butternut or harlequin squash, about 450 g (1 lb), peeled, seeded and chopped

3 celery stalks, trimmed and chopped

1 onion, peeled and chopped

¼–1 tsp dried, minced chilis

100 g (3 ½ oz) red lentils

2 tbsp tomato purée

1.2 litres (2 pints) vegetable stock

Salt and freshly ground black pepper

Fresh coriander sprigs

Fresh grated hard cheese, such as Cheddar or Monterey Jack, to serve

Preheat the cooker on high. Melt the butter in a large pan and sauté the squash, chopped celery, onion and minced chilis for 5 minutes. Add the lentils and cook, stirring, for 2 more minutes.

Blend the tomato purée with a little of the stock, add to the pan, stir, then pour in the remaining stock. Bring to the boil, add a little seasoning, then pour or spoon into the cooking pot.

Reduce the temperature to low, cover and cook for 6 to 8 hours. When ready to serve, blend the soup until smooth, and adjust seasoning. Reheat if necessary, and serve sprinkled with a little cheese and garnished with fresh coriander sprigs.

TURKEY AND RICE CHOWDER

This chowder is a meal in itself. Use quick cooking rice as this makes a difference to the finished dish, and remember to rinse the rice first.

SERVES **6**   PREPARATION TIME **25 min**   COOKING TIME **Cook on low 5 to 7 hrs**   AUTO COOK **7 to 10 hrs**

INGREDIENTS

25 g (1 oz) unsalted butter

1 medium onion, peeled and chopped

2 garlic cloves, peeled and minced

1 green jalapeño chile, seeded and chopped

225 g (8 oz) skinned, boned turkey breast steak, finely chopped

50 g (1 ¾ oz) quick cooking rice, rinsed

2 carrots, peeled and finely diced

75 g (2 ½ oz) baby corn, chopped

1 orange pepper, seeded and chopped

1 red pepper, seeded and chopped

1.2 litres (2 pints) turkey or chicken stock

Salt and freshly ground black pepper

¼ tsp fresh grated nutmeg

75 g (2 ½ oz) shelled peas, thawed if frozen

1 tbsp chopped fresh tarragon

3–5 tbsp single cream

Warm crusty bread, to serve

Preheat the cooker on high. Melt the butter in a large pan and sauté the onion, garlic and chile for 3 minutes. Add the chopped turkey and continue to sauté for another 3 minutes or until seared. Add the rice and cook for 2 minutes before adding the carrots, baby corn and peppers. Pour in the stock, add seasoning with the grated nutmeg and bring to the boil.

Pour or ladle the soup into the cooking pot, cover and reduce the temperature to low. Cook for 4 to 6 hours, then stir in the peas and continue to cook for 1 hour. Add the chopped tarragon and cream, then adjust seasoning to taste. Reheat if necessary. Serve with chunks of warm crusty bread.

RIGHT: *LENTIL AND SQUASH BROTH*

WILD MUSHROOM AND CHILE SOUP

When using dried mushrooms, it is important that they are allowed to soak in hot but not boiling water as this may impair their flavour.

SERVES **4**   PREPARATION TIME **40 min**   COOKING TIME **Cook on low 4 to 5 hrs**   AUTO COOK **5 to 8 hrs**

INGREDIENTS

1 tbsp dried porcini mushrooms

2 tbsp olive oil

1–2 fresh red jalapeño chiles, seeded and chopped

2–3 garlic cloves, peeled and chopped

4 shallots, peeled and finely chopped

225 g (8 oz) potatoes, peeled and diced

225 g (8 oz) assorted wild mushrooms, such as chanterelles, oyster, and girolles, wiped clean

100 g (3 ½ oz) sliced button mushrooms, wiped clean

1 tbsp flour

600 ml (20 fl oz) vegetable or chicken stock

Salt and freshly ground black pepper

150 ml (5 fl oz) sour cream

Flat leaf parsley sprigs, to garnish

Warm Italian bread, to serve

Soak the porcini in hot but not boiling water for at least 20 minutes and drain, reserving the liquid. Preheat the cooker on high. Heat the oil in a large pan and sauté the chile, garlic, shallots and potatoes for 5 minutes. Cut any large wild mushrooms into small pieces. Add to the pan with the drained porcini and the button mushrooms and sauté for 2 minutes. Sprinkle in the flour and cook for 2 minutes, then gradually stir in the stock. Strain the reserved soaking liquid and add to the pan with a little seasoning.

Bring to the boil, then spoon or pour into the cooking pot. Cover and reduce the temperature to low and cook for 4 to 5 hours.

Cool slightly, then blend until smooth, stir in the sour cream, and adjust seasoning to taste. Reheat if necessary. Serve, garnished with parsley and accompanied by chunks of warm Italian bread.

CHICKEN CLAM CHOWDER

The potatoes need to be completely covered with the stock to ensure that they are thoroughly cooked.

SERVES **4 to 6**   PREPARATION TIME **15 min**   COOKING TIME **Cook on low 6 to 8 hrs**   AUTO COOK **7 to 12 hrs**

INGREDIENTS

225 g (8 oz) gammon bacon, diced

1 large onion, peeled and chopped

2 celery sticks, trimmed and chopped

2 medium potatoes, peeled and diced

2 boneless, skinless chicken thighs, about 300 g (10 oz), diced

750 ml (25 fl oz) chicken stock

Salt and freshly ground black pepper

300 g (10 oz) tinned clams

175 g (6 oz) sweetcorn, thawed if frozen

6 tbsp single cream

2 tbsp chopped fresh parsley

Crusty bread or cornbread, to serve

Preheat the slow cooker on high. Place the gammon bacon in a large pan and heat gently, stirring, until the fat begins to run. Add the onion, celery and potatoes and continue to sauté for 3 minutes. Add the diced chicken and continue to cook, stirring frequently, until seared. Stir in the stock and seasoning to taste, then bring to the boil.

Pour into the cooking pot, cover and reduce the temperature to low. Cook for 5 hours. Add the clams with their juice and sweetcorn and continue to cook for 1 to 3 hours. Stir in the cream with the parsley, adjust seasoning, and serve with crusty bread or cornbread.

LEFT: *WILD MUSHROOM AND CHILE SOUP*

LEEK AND LIME VICHYSSOISE

Lemon grass imparts a distinctive citrus flavour which is similar to that of a lemon but with a slightly perfumed aroma. If unavailable, use 1 tablespoon of grated lemon zest.

SERVES **4**   PREPARATION TIME **25 min**   COOKING TIME **Cook on low 5 to 6 hrs**   AUTO COOK **6 to 8 hrs**

INGREDIENTS

2 stalks lemon grass

25 g (1 oz) unsalted butter

2 medium leeks, thoroughly washed, trimmed and sliced

2-3 garlic cloves, peeled and chopped

350 g (12 oz) potatoes, peeled and diced

1 tbsp grated lime zest

4 tbsp lime juice

950 ml (32 fl oz) vegetable or chicken stock

2 tbsp chopped fresh coriander, plus extra for serving

Salt and freshly ground black pepper

Green food colouring, optional

Toasted pita bread, to serve

Preheat the cooker on high. Discard the outer leaves from the lemon grass stalks and finely chop the inner part. Melt the butter in a large pan and sauté the lemon grass, leeks, garlic and potatoes for 5 minutes, stirring frequently.

Add the lime zest and juice and cook for 2 more minutes. Then stir in the stock with half the chopped coriander and a little seasoning. Bring to the boil. Transfer to the cooking pot and cover with the lid.

Reduce the temperature to low and cook for 4 to 5 hours. Add the remaining chopped coriander, then cook for another hour. Add a little green food colouring, if desired, and a little extra hot stock or water if the soup is too thick. Adjust seasoning and reheat if serving hot, and serve.

If serving chilled, chill in the fridge for at least 3 hours. Serve sprinkled with coriander and with toasted pita bread.

CHEESY BEAN DIP

This dip is best if served warm because the cheese tends to harden as it cools. It reheats in a microwave or in the slow cooker if preferred.

SERVES **6 to 8**   PREPARATION TIME **15 min**   COOKING TIME **Cook on high 1 hr**

INGREDIENTS

1 tsp oil

450 g (1 lb) tinned refried beans

6 tbsp white wine or apple juice

1-3 red jalapeño chiles, seeded and finely chopped

2-3 garlic cloves, peeled and minced

300 g (10 oz) grated Swiss cheese

Corn tortilla chips, pretzels, vegetable crudités and cubes of bread, to serve

Preheat the cooker on high. Use the oil to wipe the cooking pot, then add the refried beans with the wine or apple juice and heat in the cooker until smooth, stirring occasionally. Stir in the chiles, garlic and cheese. Cover and cook on high for 1 hour or until the cheese has melted (it will keep on low for an extra 2 to 4 hours if not needed immediately). Stir until the mixture is smooth. Scrape down the sides of the cooker, then, if not serving immediately, reduce the temperature to low. Serve with the chips, pretzels, vegetable crudités, and bread

RIGHT: *LEEK AND LIME VICHYSSOISE*

FARMHOUSE TERRINE

Before starting to prepare this terrine, check that the dish you are using will fit comfortably in the cooking pot of your slow cooker.

MAKES **10 to 12 slices**   PREPARATION TIME **25 min**   COOKING TIME **Cook on high 5 to 6 hrs**

INGREDIENTS

150 g (5 oz) bacon

1 tsp unsalted butter

3 garlic cloves, peeled and minced

1 small onion, peeled and finely chopped

100 g (3 ½ oz) lamb liver, chopped

350 g (12 oz) pork mince

50 g (1 ¾ oz) soft white bread crumbs

2 tbsp chopped fresh mixed herbs

1 tbsp grated lemon zest

Salt and freshly ground black pepper

1 large egg, beaten

2 tbsp brandy

Salad leaves or fresh herbs, to garnish

Melba toast and cranberry sauce, to serve

Preheat the cooker on high. Take a 1.2-litre (2-pint) round pan or container that will sit in the cooking pot. Stretch the bacon rashers with the back of a knife, then use to line the pan or container, allowing the bacon rashers to fall over the sides.

Heat the butter in a pan and gently sauté the garlic and onion for 3 minutes. Add the liver and pork mince and cook for another 3 minutes or until seared all over.

Remove from the heat and stir in the bread crumbs, herbs and the lemon zest, with seasoning to taste. Mix lightly, then add the egg and brandy and mix well.

Spoon into the bacon-lined pan, pressing the mixture down, then fold the bacon over the filling. Cover with aluminium foil. Place in the cooking pot and pour boiling water around the pan to come nearly to the top of the pot. Cook on high for 5 to 6 hours. Remove, cool before turning out and garnish with salad leaves or herbs. Serve on Melba toast, spread with cranberry sauce.

CLASSIC RAGU SAUCE

This classic sauce can be used with freshly cooked spaghetti or tagliatelle, or as a basis for lasagne or cannelloni. Sprinkle with freshly chopped oregano or marjoram and freshly grated parmesan.

SERVES **4**   PREPARATION TIME **20 min**   COOKING TIME **Cook on high 3 to 4 hrs**   AUTO COOK **4 to 8 hrs**

INGREDIENTS

450 g (1 lb) beef mince

1 tbsp oil

1 medium onion, peeled and chopped

2-4 garlic cloves, peeled and minced

2 celery stalks, trimmed and chopped

2 medium carrots, peeled and diced

450 g (1 lb) tinned chopped tomatoes

2 tbsp tomato purée

1 tsp mixed dried herbs

300 ml (10 fl oz) red wine

Salt and freshly ground black pepper

Preheat the slow cooker on high. In a nonstick frying pan, sauté the beef mince for 5 minutes, until browned. Break up any lumps, remove from the heat and drain off any excess fat through a colander. Add the oil to the frying pan and sauté the onion, garlic, celery, and carrots for 3 minutes.

Return the beef to the pan, add the remaining ingredients, stir well and bring to the boil. Pour into the cooking pot of the cooker, cover and cook on high for 3 to 4 hours. Adjust seasoning and use as required.

LEFT: *FARMHOUSE TERRINE*

BLACK BEAN CHILE DIP

This recipe also makes an excellent filling for tacos, with lettuce and cucumber, topped with sour cream, salsa and grated cheese.

SERVES **6** | PREPARATION TIME **20 min, plus overnight soaking** | COOKING TIME **Cook on low 8 to 10 hrs** | AUTO COOK **10 to 14 hrs**

INGREDIENTS

225 g (8 oz) dried black beans, soaked overnight

1 tbsp sunflower oil

1 large onion, peeled and chopped

2–4 garlic cloves, peeled and chopped

1–3 red serrano chiles, seeded and chopped

1 large carrot, peeled and diced

1 red pepper, seeded and chopped

450 g (1 lb) tinned chopped tomatoes

175 ml (6 fl oz) vegetable stock

Salt and freshly ground black pepper

Hot chili sauce, to taste

2 tbsp chopped fresh coriander

Warm pita bread strips

Cover the black beans with cold water and leave to soak overnight. The next day, preheat the cooker on high. Drain the beans, place in a large pan, cover with cold water and bring to the boil. Boil steadily for 10 minutes, then drain and place in the cooking pot. Heat the oil in a frying pan and sauté the onion, garlic and chiles for 3 minutes. Remove from the heat, and stir in the remaining ingredients except the seasoning, hot chili sauce and freshly chopped coriander. Stir well, then spoon into the cooking pot of the cooker.

Cook on low for 8 to 10 hours. If necessary, strain off any excess liquid, then mash the beans to form a chunky consistency. Stir in the seasoning and hot chili sauce to taste, and sprinkle with the chopped coriander. Serve with warm pita strips.

CHICKEN STOCK

Pour the prepared stock into ice cube trays and freeze. Then store in freezer bags and use as required.

SERVES **900 ml (30 fl oz)** | PREPARATION TIME **10 min** | COOKING TIME **Cook on high 2 hrs then low to 4 hrs**

INGREDIENTS

1 chicken carcass, cut into pieces

1 onion, peeled and roughly chopped

1 carrot, peeled and roughly chopped

1 celery stalk, trimmed and roughly chopped

2 bay leaves

4–6 whole cloves

10 black peppercorns

Few fresh parsley stalks

Preheat the cooker on high. Rinse the carcass pieces, removing any stuffing, skin or fat, and place in the cooking pot. Add all the other ingredients plus 950 ml (32 fl oz) of water and cover with the lid. Cook on high for 2 hours, then reduce to low and cook for another 4 hours. Strain and skim. Store covered in the fridge and use as required.

The stock can be frozen and used within 1 month. If kept in the fridge, use within 3 days but take care that the stock is boiled for at least 3 minutes. To make a vegetable stock, omit the chicken carcass and increase the amount of vegetables. Do not use vegetables such as potatoes, which break up, or cabbage, which has a very strong flavour, as these may spoil the stock. Proceed as above.

Beef stock can also be made in the same way – break the bones if necessary, and if raw, brown in a frying pan. Proceed as above.

RIGHT: *BLACK BEAN CHILE DIP*

SPICY SQUASH SOUP

This soup reminds me of autumn, with its rich golden coloured leaves. It is low in fat and deliciously spicy and warming as the days get colder.

SERVES **6 to 8**   PREPARATION TIME **10 min**   COOKING TIME **Cook on high 3 to 4 hrs**

INGREDIENTS

1 large butternut squash, peeled, halved and seeded

1 large carrot, peeled and chopped

2 tbsp vegetable oil

1 large onion, thinly sliced

1 clove garlic, crushed

1 tsp peeled and finely chopped ginger

½ tsp ground cumin

½ tsp ground coriander

½ tsp garam masala

950 ml (32 fl oz) vegetable stock

Salt and freshly ground black pepper

Crème fraîche, to serve

Freshly chopped chives, to serve

Cut the squash into large cubes, and place in the slow cooker with the carrot. Heat the vegetable oil in a large saucepan, add the onion, garlic, ginger, and spices. Stir well. Cover and cook for about 10 minutes, over medium heat, stirring occasionally and checking that the spices do not burn. Add the stock and bring to the boil for a few minutes.

Transfer to the cooking pot, and season to taste. Cook on high for 3 to 4 hours. If you like a smooth-textured soup, purée in a blender or in the slow cooker with an immersion blender.

Taste for seasoning, and adjust if necessary. Serve with a little crème fraîche and sprinkle with freshly chopped chives.

CREAMY MUSHROOM SAUCE

This sauce will be perfect to serve with poached chicken or fish; alternatively, use as the basis for a pasta dish such as lasagne or cannelloni.

MAKES **750 ml (25 fl oz)**   PREPARATION TIME **15 min**   COOKING TIME **Cook on low 4 to 6 hrs**   AUTO COOK **6 to 9 hrs**

INGREDIENTS

25 g (1 oz) unsalted butter

2 large shallots, peeled and chopped

1 serrano chile, seeded and chopped

2–4 garlic cloves, peeled and minced

450 g (1 lb) mushrooms, wiped and finely chopped

475 ml (16 fl oz) vegetable stock

2 tbsp cornflour

Salt and freshly ground black pepper

3–4 tbsp single cream

Coriander, to serve

Preheat the cooker on high. Melt the butter in a large pan and sauté the shallots, chile and garlic for 3 minutes. Add the mushrooms and continue to sauté for 3 more minutes. Spoon into the cooking pot and pour over the vegetable stock. Blend the cornflour with 2 tablespoons of water and stir into the pot. Add the seasoning. Cover and cook on low for 4 hours. Adjust seasoning, stir in the cream, sprinkle with coriander and use as required, reheating if necessary.

TANGY TOMATO SAUCE

A more concentrated sauce can be made by reducing the amount of wine or stock. There is no danger of the pot boiling dry when you use the slow cooker to make sauces or stock.

MAKES **750 ml (25 fl oz)**   PREPARATION TIME **10 min**   COOKING TIME **Cook on high 3 to 5 hrs**   AUTO COOK **5 to 8 hrs**

INGREDIENTS

1 tbsp sunflower oil

1 onion, peeled and chopped

2–4 garlic cloves, peeled and minced

1–2 serrano chiles, seeded and chopped

450 g (1 lb) chopped and seeded ripe tomatoes

2 tbsp tomato purée

2 tsp Worcester sauce

475 ml (16 fl oz) red wine or stock

1 tsp brown sugar

Salt and freshly ground black pepper

1 tsp mixed dried herbs

Preheat the cooker on high. Heat the oil in a frying pan and sauté the onion, garlic and chiles for 3 minutes, then place in the cooking pot. Add all the remaining ingredients and stir well. Cover with the lid and cook on low for 4 hours. Stir well. If a smoother sauce is preferred, purée in a blender or in the slow cooker with a handheld blender, then strain. Use as directed in recipes.

RIGHT: *CREAMY MUSHROOM SAUCE*

FISH AND SEAFOOD

It can be quite difficult to cook fish in a slow cooker. Because of the delicate nature of fish, it can sometimes dry out and fall apart. Several firm-fleshed fish, however, like monkfish and salmon, cook very well in a slow cooker.

PLAICE WITH ARTICHOKE AND CAPER DRESSING

Slice the potatoes thin and ensure that the liquid covers them. Root vegetables take longer to cook in the slow cooker than fish.

SERVES	4	PREPARATION TIME	20 min	COOKING TIME	Cook on low 2 to 3 hrs	AUTO COOK	2 hrs

INGREDIENTS

- 4 large or 8 small plaice fillets
- 1 tbsp unsalted butter
- 2 small shallots, peeled and chopped
- 40 g (1 ½ oz) button mushrooms, finely chopped
- 2 tsp grated lemon zest
- 40 g (1 ½ oz) soft bread crumbs
- Salt and freshly ground black pepper
- 1 tbsp chopped fresh tarragon
- 1 egg yolk, beaten
- 150 ml (5 fl oz) orange juice or white wine
- 450 g (1 lb) new potatoes, scrubbed and sliced thin
- 425 g (15 oz) tinned artichoke hearts, drained and halved
- 2 large tomatoes, sliced
- 2 tbsp capers
- Fresh tarragon, to garnish
- Green salad, or vegetables, to serve

Preheat the slow cooker on high. Skin the plaice fillets if necessary and reserve. Heat the butter in a small pan and sauté the shallots for 2 minutes, then add the mushrooms and continue to sauté for 1 minute. Remove from the heat and stir in the lemon zest, bread crumbs, seasoning and tarragon. Mix well, then bind together with the egg yolk and a little orange juice or wine, if necessary. Place the fish skinned side down and divide the stuffing between the fillets. Roll up and secure with a cocktail stick.

Place the sliced potatoes, artichoke hearts and tomatoes in the base of the cooking pot and scatter with the capers. Place the stuffed fillets on top, then pour over the orange juice or wine. Cover and reduce the heat to low, then cook for 2 to 3 hours. Garnish with tarragon and serve with a green salad or vegetables.

BARBECUED TUNA

Choose any firm fish for this dish – swordfish or monkfish would work well. Choose the freshest-looking fish available.

SERVES	4	PREPARATION TIME	10 min	COOKING TIME	Cook on low 3 to 4 hrs

INGREDIENTS

- 1 green pepper, seeded and chopped
- 1 onion, peeled and finely chopped
- 1–2 garlic cloves, peeled and minced
- ½–1 tsp dried minced chiles
- 1 tbsp Worcester sauce
- 2 tbsp dark raw sugar
- 3 tbsp wine vinegar
- 2 tsp American mustard
- 150 ml (5 fl oz) tomato juice
- Hot pepper sauce, to taste
- 4 tuna steaks, each about 150 g (5 oz)
- Fresh coriander sprigs, to garnish

Preheat the cooker on high. Blend all the ingredients together except for the fish and herbs in a pan and bring to the boil. Remove from the heat and stir until blended. Lightly rinse the fish steaks, then place in the cooking pot. Pour over the barbecue sauce and cover with the lid. Cook on low for 3 to 4 hours, then serve with the sauce garnished with the fresh coriander sprigs.

LEFT: *Swordfish with Orange and Mango Salsa (page 46)*

SALMON WITH SWEET CHILE GLAZE

This recipe will quickly become a firm favourite. The sweet chile glaze really brings out the delicate flavours of the salmon. Try it for yourself and you'll see why.

SERVES 4	PREPARATION TIME 5 min	COOKING TIME Cook on low 2 to 3 hrs	AUTO COOK 2 hrs

INGREDIENTS

4 salmon steaks

1 serrano chile, seeded and chopped

1 garlic clove, peeled and minced

2 tbsp brown sugar

1 tbsp light soy sauce

2 tsp lime zest

2 tbsp lime juice

2–3 tsp sweet chili sauce

1 tbsp honey, optional

Fresh coriander sprigs and lime wedges, to garnish

Cooked white and wild rice, to serve

Preheat the slow cooker on high while preparing the ingredients. Lightly rinse the salmon and place in the cooking pot. Blend the remaining ingredients, except for the honey and garnishes and pour over the salmon steaks. Cover with the lid, reduce the temperature to low, and cook for 2 to 3 hours. If a slightly stickier glaze is preferred, pour the cooking liquid into a small pan, add the honey and boil vigorously for 3 minutes, then pour over the salmon. Garnish and serve with cooked rice.

MONKFISH WITH FLORENCE FENNEL

The firm, white flesh of monkfish is so meaty that it is one of the few fish that can be slow-cooked without any danger of spoiling. Monkfish may also be sold under its alternative name – angler fish.

SERVES 4	PREPARATION TIME 15 min	COOKING TIME Cook on low 3 to 4 hrs	AUTO COOK 3 to 4 hrs

INGREDIENTS

675 g (1½ lb) monkfish, central bone removed

1 Florence fennel (finocchio) bulb, trimmed and cut into wedges

1 red onion, peeled and cut into wedges

1 orange pepper, seeded and cut into wedges

1 red pepper, seeded and cut into wedges

1 tbsp Thai plum sauce

2 tbsp light soy sauce

8 tbsp orange juice

2 tsp honey

½ tsp Thai 7 spice seasoning

Fennel fronds or fresh herbs, to garnish

Cooked rice mixed with chopped fresh coriander, to serve

Preheat the slow cooker on high while preparing the ingredients. Lightly rinse the fish, pat dry, then cut into bite-size pieces and set aside. Arrange the fennel, onion and pepper wedges in the base of the cooking pot, then place the fish on top.

Blend the remaining ingredients together and pour over the fish and vegetables. Cover with the lid, reduce the temperature to low and cook for 3 to 4 hours. Serve garnished with fennel fronds or fresh herbs accompanied by coriander-flavoured rice.

RIGHT: *Salmon with Sweet Chile Glaze*

TROUT WITH PEPPERS

Peppers are so easy to skin. Cut in half, then place skin-side up under a preheated grill and cook until the skins are charred. Remove and place in a paper bag for 10 minutes, then skin.

SERVES	4	PREPARATION TIME	25 min	COOKING TIME	Cook on low 2 to 3 hrs	AUTO COOK	2 hrs

INGREDIENTS

1 tsp unsalted butter

8 small trout fillets

Salt and freshly ground black pepper

$\frac{1}{4}$–$\frac{1}{2}$ tsp dried minced chilis

1 red pepper, skinned and sliced

1 yellow pepper, skinned and sliced

1 shallot, peeled and sliced

1 small orange, sliced

150 ml (5 fl oz) white wine and water mixed together

1 tbsp slivered almonds, toasted

Fresh snipped chives, to garnish

Preheat the slow cooker on high and smear the inside with the butter. Skin the fillets, check that all the bones have been removed, especially the very fine pin bones. Rinse lightly and pat dry with kitchen roll. Place the fillets skinned-side down and season lightly with salt and pepper. Sprinkle with a little minced chili. Place 2 to 3 strips of each pepper on top of each fillet, then roll up and secure with cocktail sticks.

Place the shallot and orange in the base of the cooking pot with the stuffed fillets on top. Pour over the wine and water. Cover, reduce the temperature to low and cook for 2 to 3 hours. Remove the cocktail sticks, scatter with the almonds and garnish with the snipped chives.

SPICY SWORDFISH WITH COCONUT

This recipe will work equally well with salmon, tuna or any other fresh fish fillets. Smoked fish, however, would not combine well with the flavours used.

SERVES	4	PREPARATION TIME	15 min	COOKING TIME	Cook on low 2 to 3 hrs	AUTO COOK	2 hrs

INGREDIENTS

1 tbsp sunflower oil

1 tsp cumin seeds

1 red serrano chile, seeded and chopped

1 garlic clove, peeled and minced

1 stalk lemon grass, outer leaves discarded and chopped

1 tbsp grated lime zest

2 tbsp light soy sauce

1 tsp Thai fish sauce

150 ml (5 fl oz) coconut milk

4 swordfish steaks

1 tbsp chopped fresh coriander

Cooked sticky jasmine rice, to serve

Preheat the slow cooker on high while preparing the ingredients. Heat the oil in a frying pan and gently fry the cumin seeds, chile, garlic and lemon grass for 3 minutes, then drain on kitchen roll. Blend with the grated lime zest, soy, fish sauce and the coconut milk and set aside.

Lightly rinse the swordfish and place in the cooking pot. Pour over the coconut milk mixture and cover with the lid.

Reduce the temperature to low and cook for 2 to 3 hours. Serve sprinkled with the chopped coriander accompanied by sticky jasmine rice.

LEFT: *TROUT WITH PEPPERS*

FISH PROVENÇAL

When cooking fish in the slow cooker, it is best to skin it first. Slip a long sharp knife under the skin at the tail end, then slip it down the length of the fish, or if the fish is firm-fleshed, rip the skin off.

SERVES **4**   PREPARATION TIME **10 min**   COOKING TIME **Cook on low 3 to 4 hrs**   AUTO COOK **3 to 4 hrs**

INGREDIENTS

4 cod or other firm white fish fillets, about 560 g (1 ¼ lb)

1 onion, peeled and sliced

1 yellow pepper, seeded and sliced

425 g (15 oz) tinned artichoke hearts, drained and cut in half

4 firm tomatoes, sliced

50 g (1 ¾ oz) stoned black olives

1 bay leaf

Salt and freshly ground black pepper

120 ml (4 fl oz) medium dry white wine

Snipped fresh chives, to garnish

Warm crusty bread or new potatoes and salad, to serve

Preheat the slow cooker on high. Skin the fish if necessary, cut into bite-size pieces, and place in the cooking pot. Add the remaining ingredients except for the wine and parsley. Bring the wine to just below boiling point, pour over the fish, then cover with the lid.

Reduce the temperature to low and cook for 3 to 4 hours. Serve garnished with chives and warm crusty bread or new potatoes and salad.

FRESH SALMON MOUSSE

Chop the fish really fine for this mousse so that the fish is evenly distributed throughout. Serve with a tossed green salad and melba toast for a delicious summer lunch.

SERVES **6 to 8**   PREPARATION TIME **20 min**   COOKING TIME **Cook on low 5 to 6 hrs**

INGREDIENTS

50 g (1 ¾ oz) unsalted butter

50 g (1 ¾ oz) flour

300 ml (10 fl oz) semi-skimmed milk

150 ml (5 fl oz) low-fat sour cream

Salt and freshly ground black pepper

½ tsp fresh grated nutmeg

1 tbsp chopped fresh chervil

225 g (8 oz) cod fillet, skinned and boned

450 g (1 lb) fresh salmon fillet, skinned and boned

Grated zest and juice of 1 lemon

2 medium eggs, beaten

Chervil sprigs and lemon wedges, to garnish

Melba toast, to serve

Preheat the slow cooker on high. Lightly butter a 1.2-litre (2-pint) heatproof dish and set aside. Melt the butter in a pan and sprinkle in the flour. Cook, stirring, for 2 minutes, then take off the heat and stir in the milk. Return to the heat and cook, stirring, until thickened. Remove from the heat and stir in the sour cream with seasoning, nutmeg and chervil.

Finely chop the cod and salmon by hand or in the food processor, then stir into the prepared sauce. Add the lemon zest and juice. Pour in the beaten eggs and lightly stir the mixture until it is well mixed. Spoon into the buttered dish and smooth the top. Cover with lightly buttered aluminium foil and place in the cooking pot. Pour in sufficient water to come almost to the top of the pot, cover, reduce temperature to low and cook for 5 to 6 hours. Remove, allow to cool, then chill until required. Garnish and serve with Melba toast.

RIGHT: *FISH PROVENÇAL*

SOLE WITH BACON AND APRICOTS

This recipe works best with large fillets, which are easier to stuff, but of course it is always a matter of personal taste.

SERVES 4	PREPARATION TIME 15 min	COOKING TIME Cook on low 2 to 3 hrs	AUTO COOK 3 to 5 hrs

INGREDIENTS

4 large or 8 small sole fillets, skinned

Salt and freshly ground black pepper

4 rashers bacon

12–16 ready-to-eat dried apricots

1 tbsp cornflour

240 ml (8 fl oz) orange juice

1–2 tsp maple syrup

Lime wedges, to garnish

Creamed potatoes mixed with spring onions and cooked vegetables, to serve

Preheat the cooker on high. Place the sole fillets skinned side down onto a chopping board and season lightly. Remove any excess fat from the bacon, then place on top of the fish. If using 8 small fillets, cut the bacon in half lengthwise. Cut the apricots into 3 pieces and place on top of the bacon. Roll up, starting from the tail end. Secure with cocktail sticks if necessary. Place in the cooking pot.

Blend the cornflour with the orange juice and maple syrup, bring to the boil, stirring, and pour over the sole fillets. Cover with the lid and cook on low for 2 to 3 hours. Remove from the pot, pour around the orange sauce and serve garnished with lime wedges accompanied by creamed potatoes and vegetables.

FISH AND PRAWN PAELLA

Do make sure that the peas, corn, and prawns are thoroughly thawed before adding to the paella.

SERVES 6	PREPARATION TIME 20 min	COOKING TIME Cook on low 3 to 4 hrs	AUTO COOK 2 hrs

INGREDIENTS

1 tbsp sunflower oil

1 medium onion, peeled and chopped

2–4 garlic cloves, peeled and minced

½–1 tsp dried minced chilis

450 g (1 lb) monkfish, cubed

Pinch saffron

185 g (6 ½ oz) quick cooking rice

600 ml (20 fl oz) fish or vegetable stock

1 red pepper, seeded and chopped

1 yellow pepper, seeded and chopped

3 tomatoes, seeded and chopped

Salt and freshly ground black pepper

75 g (2 ½ oz) thawed frozen peas

50 g (1 ¾ oz) thawed frozen sweetcorn

175 g (6 oz) peeled prawns, thawed if frozen

Few cooked mussels in their shells, cooked prawns, lemon wedges, and chopped fresh coriander, to garnish

Preheat the slow cooker on high. Heat the oil in a frying pan and sauté the onion, garlic and chilis for 3 minutes. Add the monkfish, saffron and rice and stir well. Pour in the stock followed by the chopped peppers, tomatoes and a little seasoning. Bring to the boil. Transfer to the cooking pot and cover with the lid.

Reduce the temperature to low and cook for 3 to 4 hours. One hour before the end of the cooking time add the peas, corn and prawns, and continue to cook. Serve garnished with the mussels, prawns, lemon wedges and chopped coriander.

LEFT: *SOLE WITH BACON AND APRICOTS*

SKATE WITH TOMATOES AND OLIVES

The flavour of any fish cooked in the slow cooker is superb. This is especially true with delicate tasting fish such as skate.

SERVES 4	PREPARATION TIME 15 min	COOKING TIME Cook on low 2 to 4 hrs	AUTO COOK 2 hrs

INGREDIENTS

4 small skate wings

2–3 tbsp plain flour

Salt and freshly ground black pepper

1 tbsp unsalted butter

550 g (1 ¼ lb) new potatoes, scrubbed and sliced thick

1 medium onion, peeled and sliced

3 medium tomatoes, peeled, seeded and chopped

1 orange pepper, seeded and sliced

50 g (1 ¾ oz) stuffed green olives

1–2 tbsp capers, drained

120 ml (4 fl oz) white wine or orange juice

1 tbsp chopped fresh basil and basil sprigs, to serve

Preheat the slow cooker on high. Rinse the skate wings and dip in the flour seasoned with salt and pepper. Heat the butter and brush a little around the cooking pot. Put the potatoes in the base of the pot, and top with the skate wings. Gently sauté the onion in the remaining butter for 3 minutes then add the remaining ingredients, except the basil, and season to taste. Pour over the skate wings, cover with the lid, reduce the temperature to low, and cook for 2 to 4 hours. Sprinkle with the basil and serve.

FISH AND PASTA BAKE

Dried pasta will give far better results when cooked in the slow cooker. Do not use fresh pasta as this will become soggy.

SERVES 4	PREPARATION TIME 15 min	COOKING TIME Cook on low 3 to 4 hrs	AUTO COOK 3 to 4 hrs

INGREDIENTS

1 tbsp unsalted butter

1 medium onion, peeled and chopped

1 small red jalapeño chile, seeded and chopped

100 g (3 ½ oz) chopped button mushrooms

450 g (1 lb) fresh tuna steaks, skinned and cut into cubes

1 ripe mango, peeled, stoned and chopped

3 tomatoes, seeded and chopped

100 g (3 ½ oz) dried pasta shapes

600 ml (20 fl oz) mango or orange juice

Salt and freshly ground black pepper

2 tbsp chopped fresh coriander, to garnish

Strips of warm pita bread, to serve

Preheat the slow cooker on high. Heat the butter in a frying pan and sauté the onion and chile for 3 minutes. Add the mushrooms and cook for another minute. Stir in the remaining ingredients except for the coriander and transfer to the cooking pot.

Cover with the lid, reduce the temperature to low and cook for 3 to 4 hours. Serve sprinkled with the coriander and with pita bread.

RIGHT: *Skate with Tomatoes and Olives*

SCALLOP, PRAWN AND SAFFRON RICE

It is preferable to use saffron strands rather than saffron powder. Either soak the strands in warm water for a few minutes, then use both the strands and soaking liquid or sprinkle straight into the dish at the beginning of cooking.

SERVES **4**   PREPARATION TIME **10 min**   COOKING TIME **Cook on low 2 to 3 hrs**

INGREDIENTS

2 tbsp unsalted butter

1 onion, peeled and chopped

2 medium leeks, trimmed and sliced

Few saffron strands

175 g (6 oz) quick cooking brown long grain rice, rinsed

300 g (10 oz) scallops, rinsed and halved if large

225 g (8 oz) large uncooked, peeled prawns

600 ml (20 fl oz) fish or chicken stock

1 orange pepper, peeled and chopped

4 tomatoes, seeded and chopped

Salt and freshly ground black pepper

2 tbsp chopped fresh parsley

2 large eggs, hard-boiled, shelled, and quartered, to garnish

Preheat the cooker on high. Wipe the cooking pot with a little of the butter, then heat the remaining butter in the frying pan and sauté the onion and leeks for 3 minutes, stirring frequently. Add the saffron and rice and continue to sauté for 2 minutes. Add the scallops and prawns and cook for 3 minutes, stirring, then add the remaining ingredients except for the parsley and eggs and bring to the boil.

Spoon into the cooking pot, cover with the lid, and cook for 2 to 3 hours. Stir, adjust the seasoning, then serve immediately sprinkled with the parsley and garnished with the hard-boiled eggs.

SWORDFISH WITH ORANGE AND MANGO SALSA

This spicy fish dish, with the citrus flavours blending with the hot jerk seasoning, is colourful and bright, and delicious served with basmati rice flavoured with a little saffron.

SERVES 4   **PREPARATION TIME** 10 min   **COOKING TIME** Cook on high 2 hrs

INGREDIENTS

60 ml (2 fl oz) extra-virgin olive oil

2 tbsp jerk seasoning

120 ml (4 fl oz) freshly squeezed lime juice

3 tbsp freshly squeezed orange juice

120 ml (4 fl oz) tequila

3 tsp freshly chopped coriander

Salt and freshly ground black pepper

4 swordfish steaks (1 steak per person)

For the orange & mango salsa:

2 ripe mangoes, peeled and diced

3 oranges, peeled and diced

100 g (3 ½ oz) sliced spring onions

3 tbsp freshly chopped coriander

½ tsp ground ginger

½ jalapeño pepper, seeded and finely chopped

Juice of ½ lime, to serve (optional)

In a bowl, mix the olive oil with the jerk seasoning, lime juice, orange juice, tequila, coriander and salt and pepper to taste. Transfer to the slow cooker, place the swordfish steaks on top, cover, and cook on low for 2 hours.

To make the salsa, combine all the ingredients in a bowl. Set aside until ready to serve.

Serve the swordfish steaks with the salsa and a squeeze of lime, if using.

DOVER SOLE WITH LEMON AND CHIVE BUTTER

Cooking fish in the slow cooker has two main advantages: the delicate flavours of the fish are intensified and the nutritional values are preserved.

SERVES 4   **PREPARATION TIME** 10 min   **COOKING TIME** Cook on low 2 to 3 hrs   **AUTO COOK** 3 to 4 hrs

INGREDIENTS

50 g (1 ¾ oz) softened butter

4 Dover or lemon sole, filleted and skinned

Salt and freshly ground black pepper

Grated zest from 1 lemon

Small bunch chives, snipped

3 tbsp lemon juice

Lemon wedges and fresh chives, to garnish

Preheat the cooker on high. Smear the cooking pot with a little of the butter. Lightly rinse and pat dry the fish fillets and place skinned side down on a chopping board. Season with salt and pepper, then sprinkle with a little grated lemon zest. Sprinkle each fillet with a few snipped chives, then roll up, starting from the head end. Place in the cooking pot. Pour the lemon juice around the fish. Dot with the remaining butter, cover and cook on low for 2 to 3 hours. Carefully remove from the pot and pour over the chive butter sauce that has formed in the pot. Garnish with lemon wedges and chives.

RIGHT: *Swordfish with Orange and Mango Salsa*

FISH CREOLE

You can vary the fish according to availability and personal taste. Choose a fish whose flavour will not be lost in the robust sauce.

....

| SERVES | **4** | PREPARATION TIME | **15 min** | COOKING TIME | **Cook on low 3 to 4 hrs** |

INGREDIENTS

1 tbsp sunflower oil

1 large onion, peeled and chopped

6 garlic cloves, peeled and minced

2 celery sticks, trimmed and chopped

2 large tomatoes, seeded and chopped

1 red pepper, seeded and finely chopped

2 tbsp tomato purée

475 ml (16 fl oz) fish or chicken stock

Few dashes hot pepper sauce

1 tbsp lime juice

1 tsp brown sugar

1 tsp dried thyme

350 g (12 oz) orange roughy fillets, skinned and cut into bite-size pieces

Salt and freshly ground black pepper

100 g (3 ½ oz) peeled prawns, thawed if frozen

1 tbsp chopped fresh thyme, to garnish

Cooked rice, to serve

Preheat the cooker on high while preparing the ingredients. Heat the oil in a large pan and sauté the onion, garlic, and celery for 3 minutes. Add the tomatoes and red pepper and stir well.

Blend the tomato purée with the stock and pour into the pan together with the hot pepper sauce, lime juice, sugar and dried thyme. Bring to the boil, then pour into the cooking pot. Add the fish with a little seasoning, cover with the lid and cook for 2 ½ hours. Add the prawns and continue to cook for an additional 30 minutes to 1 ½ hours. Adjust seasoning, then serve sprinkled with the chopped thyme accompanied by the freshly cooked rice.

TUNA WITH MANGO SALSA

This recipe, using a mango salsa, would work well with swordfish or salmon. Beat the refried beans so that they are not too lumpy.

....

| SERVES | **4** | PREPARATION TIME | **15 min** | COOKING TIME | **Cook on low 3 to 4 hrs** | AUTO COOK | **4 to 6 hrs** |

INGREDIENTS

1 tsp sunflower oil

3 tbsp white wine

425 g (15 oz) tinned refried beans

4 tuna steaks, each about 150 g (5 oz)

Salt and freshly ground black pepper

1 small ripe mango, peeled, stoned and finely chopped

4 shallots, peeled and finely chopped

1–2 green jalapeño chiles, seeded and chopped

1–2 garlic cloves, peeled and minced

3 ripe but firm tomatoes, seeded and chopped

2 tbsp chopped fresh coriander

Flat leaf parsley sprigs, to garnish

Cooked rice and salad, to serve

Preheat the cooker on high. Lightly oil the cooking pot with the sunflower oil. Place the wine and beans into the cooking pot and heat through while preparing the remaining ingredients. Lightly rinse the tuna steaks, pat dry, season and set aside. To make the mango salsa, stir together the mango, shallots, chiles, garlic, tomatoes and coriander and set aside.

Beat the refried beans in the cooking pot until smooth, then place the tuna on top of the beans. Spoon over the mango salsa, cover and cook on low for 3 to 4 hours. Garnish with parsley sprigs and serve with freshly cooked rice and a salad.

LEFT: *FISH CREOLE*

MEAT

Aslow cooker is excellent for cooking the cheaper cuts of meat. In fact, they are better than more expensive cuts. Adding good-quality stock makes a huge difference to the taste, and adding wine helps to tenderise and flavour the meat.

BRAISED BEEF

Cheaper cuts of meat are full of flavour and extremely tasty but do require long slow cooking. This is where the slow cooker comes into its own, as you do not have to use the best cut of beef when making casseroles.

| SERVES | 4 | PREPARATION TIME | 30 min | COOKING TIME | Cook on low 7 to 9 hrs | AUTO COOK | 9 to 12 hrs |

INGREDIENTS

675 g (1 ½ lb) beef bottom round or round steak, trimmed and diced

2 tbsp plain flour

Salt and fresh ground black pepper

1 tbsp sunflower oil

8 baby onions, peeled

2 garlic cloves, peeled and chopped

1 tbsp hot paprika

300 ml (10 fl oz) beef stock

1 tbsp tomato purée

4 large tomatoes, chopped

Fresh grated nutmeg, to taste

1 large red pepper, seeded and chopped

100 g (3 ½ oz) button mushrooms

Preheat the slow cooker on high. Toss the beef in the flour seasoned with salt and pepper until coated, reserving any excess flour. Heat the oil in a large pan and brown the beef on all sides; do this in batches. Remove from the pan with a slotted spoon and reserve. Cut the onions in half if large, then add to the pan with the garlic and sauté, stirring frequently, for 5 minutes. Return the beef to the pan, sprinkle in any remaining flour plus the paprika, and cook for 3 minutes. Take the pan off the heat, then gradually stir in the stock and the tomato purée blended with 2 tablespoons of water. Return to the heat and cook, stirring, until the liquid comes to the boil.

Remove from the heat and add the chopped tomatoes. Add a little seasoning with the fresh grated nutmeg, place in the cooking pot, cover, and cook on low for 5 hours. Blanch the red pepper in boiling water for 2 minutes, then drain. Slice the mushrooms in half then add to the pot with the pepper. Continue to cook for 2 to 4 hours. Adjust the seasoning and serve.

LEFT: *Beef Pot Roast (page 69)*

BOEUF BOURGUIGNON

The slow cooker cooks this classic french dish so that it simply melts in the mouth. Try it with the creamy mashed potatoes flavoured with spring onions to bring the recipe right up to date.

SERVES **4**   PREPARATION TIME **25 min, plus marinating**   COOKING TIME **Cook on low 5 to 7 hrs**   AUTO COOK **7 to 10 hrs**

INGREDIENTS

675 g (1 ½ lb) good quality beef bottom round or round steak

300 ml (10 fl oz) red wine

2 tbsp brandy

2 tbsp sunflower oil

175 g (6 oz) piece slab bacon, rind and fat removed, and diced small

8–12 baby onions, peeled

4–6 garlic cloves, peeled but left whole

3 tbsp plain flour

150 ml (5 fl oz) beef stock

Few fresh thyme sprigs

Creamy mashed potatoes flavoured with spring onions, to serve

Fresh thyme sprigs, to garnish

Preheat the slow cooker on high while preparing ingredients. (If marinating overnight, heat just before cooking.) Trim and discard any fat or gristle from the beef and cut into cubes. Place in a shallow dish and pour over the red wine and brandy. Cover and leave to marinate for at least 30 minutes, or overnight if time permits. When ready to cook, drain, reserving the marinade.

Heat the oil in a large pan and sear the beef and chopped bacon on all sides, remove and set aside. Add the whole baby onions and garlic and sauté for 5 minutes, stirring frequently. Then return the seared meat to the pan. Sprinkle in the flour and cook, stirring, for 3 minutes, then take off the heat. Gradually stir in the reserved marinade and the stock.

Bring to the boil, then transfer to the cooking pot and add the thyme sprigs. Cover, reduce the heat and cook on low for 5 to 7 hours. Adjust seasoning and serve with the spring onion flavoured mashed potatoes.

LEMON PORK WITH CUMIN

If you like crisp skin on the joint, do not brown the joint before cooking. Once cooked, remove the pork joint from the cooker and grill the skin for about 10 minutes.

SERVES **6 to 8**   PREPARATION TIME **20 min**   COOKING TIME **Cook on low 5 to 7 hrs**   AUTO COOK **8 to 10 hrs**

INGREDIENTS

1.3 kg (3 lb) pork leg joint

1 tbsp unsalted butter

1 medium onion, peeled and chopped

2–4 garlic cloves, peeled and chopped

1 tsp cumin seeds

1 large lemon, cut into wedges

150 ml (5 fl oz) dry white wine

300 ml (10 fl oz) vegetable or chicken stock

1 tbsp soy sauce

Few fresh sage leaves

1 tbsp cornflour

Preheat the slow cooker on high. Discard the rind and excess fat from the pork. Heat the butter in a frying pan, sear the pork on all sides, and place in the cooking pot. Add the onion, garlic, and cumin to the frying pan and sauté for 3 minutes, stirring frequently. Add the lemon wedges to the pan and continue to sauté for 3 minutes. Spoon over the pork joint. Blend the wine, stock, and soy sauce and pour over the joint; then add the sage leaves. Cover with a lid, reduce the heat to low, and cook for 5 to 7 hours. Remove the joint from the pot and keep warm. Strain the cooking liquid into a pan and bring to the boil. Blend the cornflour with 1 tablespoon of water, then stir into the boiling stock. Cook, stirring frequently, until thickened and smooth.

RIGHT: *BOEUF BOURGUIGNON*

BEEF AND HORSERADISH SANDWICH

When cooking whole joints, check that the joint will fit in the slow cooking pot and that the lid fits properly, otherwise the cooker will not work efficiently.

SERVES **4 to 6**   PREPARATION TIME **5 min**   COOKING TIME **Cook on high 3 to 5 hrs**

INGREDIENTS

900 g (2 lb) beef joint such as chuck

1 tbsp creamed horseradish sauce

1 tbsp Worcester sauce

3 tbsp tomato ketchup

1 tbsp balsamic vinegar

2 tbsp maple syrup

Large warm rolls, rocket, sliced red onion sliced large tomatoes, with assorted relishes and pickles, to serve

Preheat the slow cooker on high. Wipe the joint and place in the slow cooker cooking pot. Blend the horseradish and Worcester sauce with the tomato ketchup, balsamic vinegar, maple syrup and 4 tablespoons of water, then pour over the joint. Cover and cook on high for 3 to 5 hours.

Remove and allow to cool slightly before slicing and serving on rolls with the rocket, sliced red onion, sliced tomatoes and assorted relishes and pickles.

CHILI CON CARNE

If preferred, you can use chuck steak cut into small pieces in place of the beef mince.

SERVES **4**   PREPARATION TIME **25 min**   COOKING TIME **Cook on low 8 to 10 hrs**   AUTO COOK **9 to 12 hrs**

INGREDIENTS

450 g (1 lb) beef mince

1 tsp sunflower oil

1 medium onion, peeled and chopped

2-3 red jalapeño chiles, seeded and chopped

2-4 garlic cloves, peeled and minced

2 celery sticks, trimmed and chopped fine

450 g (1 lb) ripe tomatoes, peeled and chopped

2 tbsp tomato purée

2 tbsp chopped fresh coriander

Salt and fresh ground black pepper

410 g (14 ½ oz) tinned red kidney beans, drained and rinsed

100 g (3 ½ oz) sweetcorn, thawed if frozen

Cooked rice, grated Monterey Jack cheese, sour cream, hot chili sauce, pickled jalapeño chiles and tortilla chips, to serve

Preheat the slow cooker on high. Place the beef mince in a frying pan and heat gently, stirring frequently, until the beef is seared and any fat has run out. Drain the beef in a colander and set aside. Wipe the pan clean.

Heat the oil in the cleaned frying pan and sauté the onion, chiles, garlic and celery for 5 minutes or until beginning to soften. Return the beef mince to the pan, then stir in the chopped tomatoes.

Blend the tomato purée with 6 tablespoons of water, then stir into the beef mixture with 1 tablespoon of the chopped coriander, seasoning and the red kidney beans.

Pour into the cooking pot, cover and reduce the temperature to low. Cook for 7 to 9 hours, then stir in the corn and continue to cook for 1 hour.

Adjust the seasoning and sprinkle over the reserved coriander. Serve with rice, cheese, sour cream, hot chili sauce, pickled chiles and tortilla chips.

LEFT: *Beef and Horseradish Sandwich*

CHILI TACOS

This filling would also be great if used to make enchiladas or tostadas. Make a double batch and freeze half for later.

SERVES **6**   PREPARATION TIME **15 min**   COOKING TIME **Cook on low 3 to 4 hrs**   AUTO COOK **4 to 6 hrs**

INGREDIENTS

450 g (1 lb) beef mince

1 tbsp sunflower oil

1 large onion, peeled and chopped fine

2–4 garlic cloves, peeled and minced

2 celery sticks, trimmed and chopped

1–2 tsp hot chili powder, to taste

$\frac{1}{2}$ tsp ground cinnamon

$\frac{1}{2}$ tsp ground coriander

$\frac{1}{2}$ tsp ground cloves

1 green pepper, seeded and chopped fine

410 g (14 $\frac{1}{2}$ oz) tinned chopped tomatoes

200 g (7 oz) tinned red kidney or chickpeas, drained and rinsed

100 g (3 $\frac{1}{2}$ oz) pickled chiles, drained and chopped

150 ml (5 fl oz) beef stock

Salt and fresh ground black pepper

1 tbsp fresh chopped coriander

1 small avocado, peeled, stoned and sliced

Sour cream, lime wedges and taco shells, to serve

Preheat cooker on high. Heat a large frying pan and fry the beef, stirring frequently to break up any lumps, until seared. Remove from the heat and set aside.

Add the oil to the pan and sauté the onion, garlic and celery for 3 minutes. Add the chili powder and spices and fry for another 2 minutes, stirring frequently. Return the beef to the pan, stir, then add the remaining ingredients except for the chopped coriander and avocado. Bring to the boil, then pour into the cooking pot.

Cover with the lid and cook on low for 3 to 4 hours. If the chili mixture is too wet, remove the lid at the end of the cooking time, turn the heat up to high and cook uncovered for 20 to 30 minutes. Serve sprinkled with the chopped coriander, sliced avocado, lime wedges, sour cream and taco shells.

BLACK BEANS WITH SAUSAGE

This is a hearty dish and is great when served with plenty of freshly grated hard cheese, such as Monterey Jack or Cheddar, warm crusty bread and a tossed green salad.

SERVES	4 to 6	PREPARATION TIME	10 min, plus overnight soaking	COOKING TIME	Cook on high 6 to 8 hrs	AUTO COOK	8 to 10 hrs

INGREDIENTS

225 g (8 oz) dried black beans, soaked overnight

1 tbsp sunflower oil

1 large red onion, peeled and chopped

2-4 garlic cloves, peeled and minced

2 celery sticks, trimmed and chopped

½–1 tsp dried minced chiles

1 tsp ground cumin

1 tsp dried mustard powder

1 green pepper, seeded and chopped

8 spicy pork or Toulouse sausages

410 g (14 ½ oz) tinned chopped tomatoes

1 tbsp maple syrup

300 ml (10 fl oz) beef or chicken stock

2 fresh bay leaves

Salt and fresh ground black pepper

1 tbsp chopped fresh thyme, to garnish

Soak the black beans overnight in plenty of cold water. Next day, preheat the cooker on high while preparing the ingredients. Drain the beans, rinse and place in a large pan, cover with cold water and bring to the boil. Boil steadily for 10 minutes, then drain and place in the cooking pot. Meanwhile, heat the oil in a large frying pan and sauté the onion, garlic, and celery with the chiles, cumin, and mustard powder for 3 minutes. Add the pepper, stir well, spoon into the cooker, and stir into the beans.

Add the sausages to the pan and cook until browned all over. Remove and place on top of the bean mixture. Blend the tomatoes with the maple syrup and stock, then pour over the sausages and add the bay leaves to the pot. Cover and cook on high for 6 to 8 hours. Add seasoning to taste, sprinkle with the chopped thyme and serve.

PORK CASSOULET

This cassoulet is ideal for hearty appetites. Serve with plenty of cornbread and a tossed green salad for a satisfying and filling meal.

SERVES	4	PREPARATION TIME	20 min	COOKING TIME	Cook on low 6 to 8 hrs	AUTO COOK	10 to 12 hrs

INGREDIENTS

300 g (10 oz) Boston-style pork shoulder or butt, boned and cut into cubes

8 thick Toulouse or pork sausages

1 medium onion, peeled and chopped

3-4 garlic cloves, peeled and chopped

3 celery sticks, trimmed and chopped

1 tbsp fresh chopped marjoram

1 tbsp fresh chopped thyme

Salt and fresh ground black pepper

300 g (10 oz) tinned cannellini beans, drained and rinsed

300 g (10 oz) tinned black eye peas, drained and rinsed

410 g (14 ½ oz) tinned chopped tomatoes

50 g (1 ¾ oz) soft bread crumbs

Fresh herbs, to garnish

Preheat the slow cooker on high. Place the pork in a frying pan and heat gently until the fat begins to run out. Prick the sausages and add to the frying pan and brown all over. Remove and chop into large chunks. Add the onion, garlic, and celery to the frying pan, cook for 3 minutes, then add the chopped herbs with seasoning.

Layer the pork and onion mixture with the beans, peas and chopped sausages in the cooking pot, then pour over the chopped tomatoes with their juice. Sprinkle over the bread crumbs and cover with the lid.

Reduce the temperature to low and cook for 6 to 8 hours. Serve garnished with fresh herbs.

LEFT: *BLACK BEANS WITH SAUSAGE*

FRUITY PORK CHOPS

You will find that cooking meat in the slow cooker prevents the meat from shrinking as much as it does when cooked conventionally.

SERVES 4	PREPARATION TIME 15 min	COOKING TIME Cook on low 4 to 6 hrs	AUTO COOK 6 to 8 hrs

INGREDIENTS

4 boneless pork chops

2 carrots, peeled and cut into slices

1 medium onion, peeled and sliced

1 red pepper, seeded and sliced

75 g (2 ½ oz) ready-to-eat dried apricots

1 tbsp brown sugar

1 tbsp tomato purée

1 tsp ground cinnamon

1 tsp hot chili sauce or to taste

1 tbsp red wine vinegar

1 tbsp grated orange zest

300 ml (10 fl oz) mango or orange juice

Salt and fresh ground black pepper

1 ½ tbsp cornflour

1 large ripe mango, stoned, peeled and diced

175 g (6 oz) rough diced courgettes

Warm bread or cooked rice, to serve

Lime wedges and watercress, to garnish

Preheat the slow cooker on high. Trim off any excess fat from the chops and place in the cooking pot. Scatter over the sliced carrots, onion, pepper and dried apricots. Blend together the brown sugar, the tomato purée, ground cinnamon and hot chili sauce then stir in the vinegar and orange zest.

Blend the mango or orange juice into the sugar mixture then pour over the pork chops. Add a little seasoning. Cover with a lid and reduce the temperature to low and cook for 3 to 5 hours.

Blend the cornflour with 2 tablespoons of water, then stir into the pot with the diced mango and courgettes and cook for 1 more hour before serving with warm bread or rice, garnished with lime and watercress.

BARBECUED RIBS

The flavour of these ribs is wonderful. Make sure that you provide plenty of serviettes – you will find that everyone needs them!

SERVES 4	PREPARATION TIME 5 min	COOKING TIME Cook on high 1 hr then low 3 to 4 hrs	AUTO COOK 8 to 10 hrs

INGREDIENTS

1 medium onion, peeled and chopped fine or grated

3-4 garlic cloves, peeled and minced

1 tbsp brown sugar

4 tbsp tomato ketchup

2 tbsp maple syrup

2 tsp yellow mustard

1 tsp horseradish sauce

2 tbsp white wine vinegar

2 tbsp Worcester sauce

4 tbsp orange juice

900 g (2 lb) baby back ribs

Fresh herbs, to garnish

Potato salad, baked beans and crusty bread, to serve

Preheat the slow cooker on high. Blend all the ingredients except the ribs in a pan and stir until well blended, then bring to just below boiling point. Place the ribs in the cooking pot and pour the almost boiling sauce over the ribs. Cover and cook on high for 1 hour. Reduce the temperature of the slow cooker to low and continue to cook for 3 to 4 hours.

Remove and arrange on the serving platter and keep warm. Pour the sauce into a pan and boil vigorously until reduced by half, then pour over the ribs, garnish with fresh herbs, and serve with potato salad, baked beans and crusty bread.

RIGHT: *FRUITY PORK CHOPS*

AROMATIC PORK

This easy to make recipe takes its inspiration from the wonderful fragrant flavours of Thailand. Serve with freshly cooked sticky rice and fresh plums.

SERVES **4**　　PREPARATION TIME **20 minutes, plus 30 minutes marinating time**　　COOKING TIME **Cook on low 5 to 7 hrs**　　AUTO COOK **8 to 10 hrs**

INGREDIENTS

2 lemon grass stalks

Small piece ginger, peeled and grated

1–2 serrano chiles, seeded and chopped

1–2 star anise

2 kaffir lime leaves, chopped, or crumbled if dried

300 ml (10 fl oz) orange juice

2–3 tsp clear honey or to taste

675 g (1 ½ lb) pork tenderloin (2 whole fillets), trimmed

2 tbsp sunflower oil

4–6 shallots, peeled and cut into wedges

2–3 garlic cloves, peeled and minced

1 tbsp Thai plum sauce

Fresh plums, to garnish

Preheat the slow cooker on high. Remove and discard the outer leaves of the lemon grass and chop the inner part finely. Mix together the chopped lemon grass, ginger, chiles, star anise, lime leaves, 150 ml (5 fl oz) of the orange juice and honey.

Cut the pork fillets in half and place in a shallow dish. Rub or brush the marinade over the fillet then cover loosely and leave for at least 30 minutes in the fridge.

When ready to cook, drain the pork if necessary, reserving the marinade. Heat the oil in a frying pan and seal the pork fillet all over. Remove and place in the cooking pot. Add the shallots and garlic to the frying pan and sauté for 3 minutes. Add the marinade, stir well and cook for 1 minute; then add the remaining juice and Thai plum sauce. Bring to the boil, then pour over the pork fillet and cover with the lid.

Reduce the temperature to low and cook for 5 to 7 hours. If a thicker sauce is preferred, strain off the liquid and heat to almost boiling. Blend 2 teaspoons of cornflour with 1 tablespoon of water and stir into the boiling liquid. Cook until thickened and serve with the pork. Serve sliced, garnished with fresh plums.

PORK GOULASH

One of the main advantages of using a slow cooker is that the food can be left to slowly simmer all day and part of the evening, if need be, without any risk of burning.

SERVES **4**   PREPARATION TIME **25 min**   COOKING TIME **Cook on low 5 to 7 hrs**   AUTO COOK **7 to 9 hrs**

INGREDIENTS

675 g (1 ½ lb) lean pork, trimmed and cut into cubes

2 tbsp plain flour

Salt and fresh ground black pepper

2 tbsp sunflower oil

1 large onion, peeled and cut into wedges

2–4 garlic cloves, peeled and chopped

1 tbsp paprika

300 ml (10 fl oz) vegetable or chicken stock

150 ml (5 oz) red wine

1 tbsp tomato purée

4 medium tomatoes, skinned and chopped

1 large orange pepper, seeded and chopped

100 g (3 ½ oz) sliced button mushrooms

4 tbsp sour cream

2 tbsp snipped fresh chives

Cooked rice and a tossed green salad, to serve

Preheat the slow cooker on high. Toss the pork in the flour seasoned with salt and black pepper, reserving any excess flour. Heat the oil in a large pan and sauté the onion and garlic for 3 minutes. Remove from the pan with a slotted spoon and place in the cooking pot.

Add the flour-coated pork to the pan, sear on all sides, then sprinkle in any remaining flour and the paprika. Cook for 2 minutes. Take off the heat and gradually stir in the stock and the red wine. Add the tomato purée, chopped tomatoes and a little seasoning. Bring to the boil, stirring, then pour over the onions and garlic in the cooking pot and mix together. Cover, reduce the temperature to low and cook for 4 to 6 hours.

Cover the pepper and sliced mushrooms with boiling water, leave for 5 minutes, then drain and add to the cooking pot and continue to cook for 1 more hour. Stir well, then serve topped with the sour cream and sprinkled with the chives and accompanied by the freshly cooked rice and tossed green salad.

SWEET AND SOUR HAM

It is a good idea to soak smoked ham joints overnight as this helps to remove any excess salt. It is not necessary to soak unsmoked ham, although many believe that this improves the finished flavour.

SERVES **6 to 8**   PREPARATION TIME **10 min**   COOKING TIME **Cook on high 3 to 5 hrs**

INGREDIENTS

1.8 kg (4 lb) ham joint, soaked overnight if preferred

4 whole cloves

1 cinnamon stick, bruised

300 ml (10 fl oz) orange juice

2 tbsp balsamic or red wine vinegar

1 tbsp maple syrup or clear honey

50 g (1 ¾ oz) dried bread crumbs, optional

100 g (3 ½ oz) raw sugar

1 tbsp cornflour

Cooked rice or potatoes and vegetables, to serve

Chopped fresh herbs, to garnish

Preheat the cooker on high while preparing ingredients. Drain the ham, if soaked overnight, then place in a large pan, cover with cold water and bring to the boil. Drain, rinse and place in the cooking pot with the cloves and cinnamon stick.

Blend the orange juice with the vinegar and maple syrup or honey and bring to the boil. Pour over the ham, then cover with the lid and cook on high for 3 to 5 hours.

Once cooked, remove from the cooker, and reserve the cooking liquid. Then cool the joint slightly and remove the zest. Either sprinkle with the bread crumbs or score the fat and press the raw sugar onto the fat. Place in a preheated hot oven, 200°C (400°F) and cook for 15 to 20 minutes to crisp the topping.

Pour 300 ml (10 fl oz) of the reserved cooking liquid into a small pan and bring to the boil. Blend the cornflour with 2 tablespoons of water or extra orange juice and pour into the boiling liquid. Cook, stirring, until the mixture thickens slightly, then pour over the ham, sprinkle with chopped fresh herbs and serve with either freshly cooked rice or potatoes and vegetables.

BEEF POT ROAST

Few foods satisfy as completely as a beef pot roast. The delicious flavour and the ease of cooking all the vegetables and meat in one pot is hard to beat.

SERVES **6**   PREPARATION TIME **30 min**   COOKING TIME **Cook on low 8 to 10 hrs**

INGREDIENTS

1.3 kg (3 lb) boneless beef chuck

2 tbsp olive oil

Salt and freshly ground black pepper

2 large onions, thinly sliced

3 cloves garlic, crushed

3 tbsp tomato purée

350 ml (12 fl oz) white wine

4 carrots, peeled and sliced

475 ml (16 fl oz) good-quality beef stock

1 beef stock cube

3 tbsp Worcester sauce

3 sprigs fresh thyme

410 g (14 ½ oz) tinned butter beans

Pat the beef dry with kitchen roll, rub both sides with the olive oil, and season generously with salt and freshly ground black pepper. Place a large heavy-based frying pan over high heat and sear the meat until a dark crust forms on one side, 3–5 minutes. Turn and sear the other side. Remove from the pan and set aside.

Lower the heat and add the onions and garlic to the frying pan. Cook for 5 minutes until softened, add the tomato purée and wine, and bring to the boil. Simmer until the wine has reduced by half, scraping the bottom of the pan to deglaze. Transfer to the slow cooker, add the carrots and then place the beef on top of the vegetables.

Add the beef stock, stock cube, Worcester sauce and thyme. Cover and cook on low for 8–10 hours.

Thirty minutes before the end of the cooking time, taste, adjust the seasoning if necessary and add the butter beans. Before serving, remove the thyme if you can find it.

LAMB HOT POT

Do not peek. The more you raise the lid, the longer the cooking time! Removing the lid adds about 15 minutes to the overall cooking time.

SERVES **4**   PREPARATION TIME **10 min**   COOKING TIME **Cook on low 8 to 10 hrs**   AUTO COOK **10 to 12 hrs**

INGREDIENTS

8–12 loin lamb chops

4 large sweet potatoes, peeled and sliced thin

2 medium onions, peeled and sliced

2 large carrots, peeled and sliced

4 celery stalks, trimmed and sliced

410 g (14 ½ oz) tinned cannellini beans, rinsed and drained

2 large courgettes, trimmed

Salt and fresh ground black pepper

1 tsp dried mixed herbs

410 g (14 ½ oz) tinned chopped tomatoes

75 g (2 ½ oz) stoned black olives

150 ml (5 fl oz) lamb or beef stock

1 tbsp unsalted butter, melted

Preheat the slow cooker on high. Trim any excess fat from each chop. Reserve a few sweet potatoes in a bowl of cold water. Place a layer of sliced sweet potatoes in the base of the cooking pot and top with a little sliced onion, carrot and celery. Place a layer of chops on top, with a few beans and courgette slices. Continue layering until all the vegetables and beans have been used, except for the reserved sweet potatoes, sprinkling each layer with salt, pepper and mixed herbs. Pour over the tin of tomatoes. Add the olives, then pour over the stock. Drain the remaining sweet potatoes and arrange on top. Cover, then reduce the temperature to low and cook for 8 to 10 hours. Brush the potatoes with the melted butter. Brown under a preheated grill and serve.

LEFT: *BEEF POT ROAST*

LAMB FILLET WITH PLUM SAUCE

This recipe is so simple to prepare and it is absolutely delicious. It will certainly become an all-time favourite.

SERVES **6**   PREPARATION TIME **5 min**   COOKING TIME **Cook on low 6 to 8 hrs**   AUTO COOK **8 to 10 hrs**

INGREDIENTS

2 whole lamb fillets, about 675 g (1 ½ lb)

2 tsp olive oil

2 tbsp Thai plum sauce

4 tbsp plum conserve

1 tbsp light soy sauce

1 tbsp balsamic vinegar

240 ml (8 fl oz) orange juice

1 tbsp cornflour

Flat-leaf parsley and fresh sliced plums, to garnish

Cooked noodles, to serve

Preheat the slow cooker on high. Trim the lamb fillets, heat the olive oil in a large frying pan and sear the fillets on all sides, remove from the pan and set aside.

Blend the Thai plum sauce with the plum conserve, the soy sauce, and vinegar and heat gently. Brush over the top of each fillet, then place the fillets in the cooking pot. Pour over the orange juice, then spoon over any remaining plum sauce.

Cover with the lid, reduce the temperature and cook for 6 to 8 hours or until tender. Remove the fillets and keep warm. Strain the remaining sauce in the cooking pot into a small pan and boil until slightly reduced. Blend the cornflour with 2 tablespoons of water, stir into the sauce and cook, stirring, until thickened. Slice the fillets, arrange on individual serving plates, drizzle with a little sauce and garnish with the parsley and plums. Serve with freshly cooked noodles.

LAMB WITH TAPENADE CRUST

This tapenade can be used as a dip as well as a stuffing for the lamb.

SERVES **6 to 8**   PREPARATION TIME **15 min**   COOKING TIME **Cook on high 5 to 7 hrs**

INGREDIENTS

150 g (5 oz) stoned black olives

2 tbsp capers, drained

1 tbsp freshly chopped thyme

2 garlic cloves, peeled and minced

1 tsp yellow mustard

50 g (1 ¾ oz) tinned anchovy fillets

2 tbsp brandy

2–3 tbsp olive oil

50 g (1 ¾ oz) soft bread crumbs

1 small leg of lamb, boned

2 large onions, peeled and sliced

300 ml (10 fl oz) tomato juice

Blend the olives, capers, thyme, garlic, mustard and anchovies with the anchovy oil in a food processor to form a thick paste. Gradually add the brandy with 1 tablespoon of the oil and the bread crumbs and mix together. Put the lamb on a chopping board and place half of the prepared tapenade in the centre. Fold the meat over to completely encase the stuffing, and either tie or sew the lamb together.

Preheat the slow cooker on high. Heat the remaining olive oil in a large frying pan and brown the lamb on all sides. Add the onions to the oil remaining in the frying pan and sauté for 3 minutes. Drain thoroughly and place in the cooking pot. Spread the remaining tapenade over the top of the lamb and place on top of the onions. Pour the tomato juice around the meat, cover and cook on high for 5 to 7 hours or until the lamb is tender. Serve with the braised onions.

RIGHT: *LAMB FILLET WITH PLUM SAUCE*

BRAISED LAMB SHANKS

Make sure that your cooker is large enough for the shanks to fit in comfortably. If it is not, use neck fillet rather than shanks.

SERVES **4**   PREPARATION TIME **20 min**   COOKING TIME **Cook on low 8 to 10 hrs**

INGREDIENTS

2–4 small lamb shanks, depending on size

2 tbsp plain flour

1 tbsp sunflower oil

1 large onion, peeled and chopped

2–4 garlic cloves, peeled and chopped

2 celery stalks, trimmed and chopped

450 g (1 lb) ripe tomatoes, chopped

75 g (2 ½ oz) Kalamata olives

1 tsp dried oregano

Salt and fresh ground black pepper

240 ml (8 fl oz) red wine

Fresh thyme sprigs, to garnish

Cooked potatoes and a tossed green salad, to serve

Preheat the slow cooker on high. Wipe the lamb shanks and coat them in flour.

Heat the oil in a large frying pan and brown the shanks on all sides. Remove, and drain well before placing in the cooking pot.

Sprinkle over the chopped onion, garlic, celery, tomatoes and olives, then add the dried oregano and seasoning.

Reduce the temperature to low. Cook for 8 to 10 hours or until the meat is tender. Remove the meat and vegetables from the pot and place on a serving dish. Skim off any excess fat, garnish with thyme and serve with freshly cooked potatoes and a tossed green salad.

BEEF STROGANOFF

When cutting up the steak for this recipe, try cutting it into thin strips rather than chunks.

SERVES **4**   PREPARATION TIME **10 min**   COOKING TIME **Cook on low 6 to 8 hrs**   AUTO COOK **8 to 10 hrs**

INGREDIENTS

675 g (1 ½ lb) good quality braising steak, such as blade

2 tbsp flour

2 tbsp unsalted butter

1 large onion, peeled and sliced

2–3 garlic cloves, peeled and chopped

1 tbsp tomato purée

2 tsp yellow mustard

475 ml (16 fl oz) beef stock

2 tbsp brandy

Salt and fresh ground black pepper

Fresh grated nutmeg to taste

225 g (8 oz) portobello mushrooms, wiped and sliced

150 ml (5 fl oz) sour cream

1 tbsp chopped fresh parsley, to garnish

Creamy mashed potatoes or buttered noodles and green salad, to serve

Preheat the slow cooker on high. Trim the steak, cut into strips and toss in the flour, reserving any remaining flour. Heat 1 tablespoon of the butter in a pan and brown the beef on all sides. Remove from the pan with a slotted spoon, and place in the cooking pot. Add about half of the remaining butter to the pan and gently sauté the onion and garlic for 3 minutes. Then sprinkle in any remaining flour and cook gently for a further 2 minutes.

Blend the tomato purée and mustard with the beef stock, pour into the pan and bring to the boil, stirring. Add the brandy with the seasoning and the nutmeg, then pour over the steak and cover with the lid. Reduce the temperature to low and cook for 6 to 8 hours. One hour before the end of cooking time, heat the remaining butter and gently sauté the mushrooms, then add to the pan with the sour cream. Serve sprinkled with the parsley and with creamy mashed potatoes or freshly cooked buttered noodles and a green salad.

LEFT: *BRAISED LAMB SHANKS*

POULTRY

Poultry is lean, healthy and one of the easiest and most versatile meats to cook in the slow cooker. Game is also a good choice, as the slow cooker will tenderise and improve the cheaper meats. Use a strong stock to improve flavour.

ROSÉ CHICKEN

Rosé wine is used in this recipe, hence the name – but it will work perfectly with either red or white wine. When choosing wine for cooking, do not be tempted to use wine you would not drink.

SERVES **4**   PREPARATION TIME **20 min**   COOKING TIME **Cook on high 3 to 5 hrs**

INGREDIENTS

4 chicken portions

2 tbsp plain flour

2 tbsp unsalted butter

8–12 small onions, peeled

2–4 garlic cloves, peeled, and cut into slivers

175 g (6 oz) piece slab bacon, diced

2 tbsp brandy

240 ml (8 fl oz) rosé wine

120 ml (4 fl oz) chicken stock

2 bay leaves

1 fresh bouquet garni

Salt and fresh ground black pepper

100 g (3 ½ oz) button mushrooms

1 tbsp chopped fresh parsley

Creamed potatoes flavoured with spring onions, and green salad, to serve

Preheat the slow cooker on high. Wipe or rinse the chicken portions and pat dry with kitchen roll. Coat in the flour and reserve both any excess flour and the chicken. Heat the butter in a frying pan and sauté the onions, garlic and bacon for 3 minutes. Remove with a slotted spoon and place in the cooking pot.

Add the chicken to the butter remaining in the frying pan, sear the chicken on all sides, add the brandy, heat for 1 minute, then ignite. Once the flames have subsided, remove the chicken from the pan and place in the cooking pot.

Sprinkle in the reserved flour, cook for 2 minutes, then draw off the heat and gradually stir in the wine, then the stock. Bring to the boil and pour over the chicken. Add the bay leaves, bouquet garni and seasoning, then cover and cook on high for 2 hours.

Add the mushrooms and cook for another 1 to 3 hours. Remove the bouquet garni and bay leaves, skim off any excess fat, adjust the seasoning, sprinkle with the chopped parsley, and serve with creamed potatoes and salad.

LEFT: *TURKEY TAGINE (PAGE 88)*

CHICKEN WITH COUSCOUS AND CRANBERRY STUFFING

If a thicker sauce is preferred, blend 2 teaspoons of cornflour with 1 tablespoon of water, stir into the boiling liquid and cook, stirring until thickened.

....

| SERVES 4 | PREPARATION TIME 15 min | COOKING TIME Cook on high 4 to 6 hrs |

INGREDIENTS

4 large boneless chicken breasts

50 g (1 ¾ oz) instant couscous

25 g (1 oz) dried cranberries

2–3 spring onions, trimmed and chopped fine

25 g (1 oz) chopped pecans

1 tbsp grated orange zest

½ tsp dried tarragon

Salt and fresh ground black pepper

1 large egg yolk, beaten

300 ml (10 fl oz) orange juice

2 tbsp prepared cranberry sauce

2 tbsp light soy sauce

Fresh chopped herbs, to garnish

Freshly cooked vegetables and saffron flavoured rice, to serve

Preheat the slow cooker on high. Skin and discard the chicken skin if necessary and make a deep slit along the longest side of each breast to form a deep pocket. Place between two sheets of baking paper and gently beat with a mallet or rolling pin to flatten slightly. Take care not to tear the chicken.

Just cover the couscous with boiling water and leave until all the water has been absorbed. Stir in the dried cranberries, the spring onions, pecans, orange zest, tarragon and seasoning. Stir in sufficient egg to bind the stuffing together and use to fill each chicken pocket. Either sew with fine twine or press the edges firmly together.

Place in the cooking pot. Blend the orange juice with the cranberry sauce and soy sauce and pour over the chicken breasts. Cover and cook on high for 4 to 6 hours or until tender.

Drain off the liquid into a small pan, bring to the boil, and boil for 2 to 3 minutes or until thickened slightly. Garnish the chicken and serve with the sauce, vegetables and saffron rice.

MEXICAN CHICKEN DRUMSTICKS

The addition of chocolate to a chicken dish may sound strange, but it it is delicious. Make sure, however, you use good quality bitter chocolate as other types just will not do.

SERVES **4** PREPARATION TIME **30 min** COOKING TIME **Cook on high 3 to 5 hrs**

INGREDIENTS

4–8 chicken drumsticks, skinned

1 tbsp sunflower oil

1 tbsp unsalted butter

1 onion, peeled and chopped

2–4 garlic cloves, peeled and chopped

1 red serrano chile, seeded and chopped

1 tbsp plain flour

1 tbsp tomato purée

475 ml (16 fl oz) chicken stock

4 tomatoes, peeled and chopped

2 squares (50 g/1 ¾ oz) bitter chocolate

Salt and fresh ground black pepper

2 tbsp sesame seeds

Lime wedges, to garnish

Cooked rice and a tossed green salad, to serve

Preheat the slow cooker on high. Lightly rinse or wipe the chicken drumsticks and pat dry on kitchen roll. Heat the oil and butter in a frying pan, brown the drumsticks on all sides, drain and place in the cooking pot.

Add the onion, garlic and chile to the frying pan and sauté for 5 minutes or until softened. Sprinkle in the flour and cook for 2 minutes, then take off the heat. Blend the tomato purée with 2 tablespoons of the stock and gradually stir into the pan with the remaining stock and the chopped tomatoes. Add the chocolate with seasoning and bring to the boil. Cook, stirring, until the sauce has thickened slightly, then pour over the drumsticks. Cook on high for 3 to 5 hours. Remove from the cooker, adjust the seasoning of the sauce, then pour over the chicken. Sprinkle with the sesame seeds, garnish with lime wedges and serve with freshly cooked rice and a green salad.

CAJUN DIRTY RICE

Cajun cooking relies heavily on the seasonings used, usually paprika, which consists of sweet peppers, hot chile sauce, combined with white and black peppers, garlic, dried thyme and oregano.

SERVES **4 to 6**   PREPARATION TIME **15 min**   COOKING TIME **Cook on high 2 to 4 hrs**

INGREDIENTS

6 rashers streaky bacon, chopped

350 g (12 oz) chicken livers

225 g (8 oz) fresh pork mince

1 onion, peeled and chopped fine

2–4 garlic cloves, peeled and minced

2 celery sticks, trimmed and chopped fine

1 red pepper, seeded and chopped

900 ml (30 fl oz) chicken stock

1–2 tsp Cajun seasoning

Salt and fresh ground black pepper

¼ tsp cayenne pepper, or to taste

1 tsp paprika

225 g (8 oz) quick cooking long grain rice

6 spring onions, trimmed and chopped, to garnish

Preheat the cooker on high while preparing the ingredients. Place the bacon in a nonstick frying pan and heat gently until the fat begins to run. Meanwhile, discard any sinew or gristle from the chicken livers and chop fine. Add the livers and pork mince to the pan and cook, stirring frequently, until seared. Stir in the onion, garlic, celery and pepper and continue to cook for 3 minutes, stirring frequently.

Pour in the stock with the seasonings and rice and bring to the boil, then spoon into the cooking pot. Cover with the lid and cook on high for 2 to 4 hours. Adjust seasoning and serve sprinkled with the chopped spring onions.

CHICKEN HOT POT

If preferred, substitute the parsnips with sweet potatoes.

SERVES **4**   PREPARATION TIME **25 min**   COOKING TIME **Cook on high 2 hrs then low 3 to 6 hrs**

INGREDIENTS

450 g (1 lb) chicken thighs, skinned

2 tbsp unsalted butter

1 medium onion, peeled and sliced thin

2–4 garlic cloves, peeled and minced

1 tsp dried mixed herbs

450 g (1 lb) potatoes, peeled and sliced thin

2 large carrots, peeled and sliced

2 medium parsnips, peeled and sliced

3 celery sticks, trimmed and chopped

Salt and fresh ground black pepper

600 ml (20 fl oz) chicken stock

Fresh chopped parsley, to garnish

Preheat the slow cooker on high. Discard any fat from the chicken thighs and dice. Heat 1 tablespoon of the butter in a frying pan, sear the chicken on all sides, remove and drain on kitchen roll. Add the sliced onion and garlic to the butter remaining in the frying pan and sauté for 3 minutes. Add the herbs and mix well, then remove from the heat.

Place a layer of the potatoes in the base of the cooking pot, top with a layer of carrot, parsnip and celery; season lightly between each layer. Place the chicken thighs on top and then the onion mixture. Continue the layering of the vegetables, finishing with a layer of potatoes. Bring the stock to the boil, then pour over the chicken and vegetables. Place the cooking pot in the cooker, cover and cook for 2 hours on high. Reduce the temperature to low and continue to cook for 3 to 6 hours.

Remove the lid, melt the remaining butter and use to brush over the potatoes. Place under a preheated grill and cook for 3 to 4 minutes or until golden. Serve garnished with parsley.

RIGHT: *CAJUN DIRTY RICE*

FLORIDA CHICKEN

This recipe is truly effortless. Once in the cooker, the food simply cooks itself. All you need to add is some bread or new potatoes and a salad – and your meal is ready to take to the table.

SERVES **4**   PREPARATION TIME **15 min**   COOKING TIME **Cook on high 3 to 5 hrs**

INGREDIENTS

4 chicken quarters

1 tbsp oil

1 tbsp unsalted butter

300 ml (10 fl oz) orange juice

1 tbsp grated orange and lemon zest

2 tbsp light soy sauce

1 tbsp orange blossom honey

½–1 tsp dried minced chiles

2 tsp cornflour

Fresh herbs, to garnish

Warm crusty bread or fresh cooked new potatoes, to serve

Preheat the slow cooker on high. Wipe the chicken quarters, heat the oil and butter in a large frying pan and brown the chicken all over. Remove and drain well on kitchen roll, then arrange in the slow cooker cooking pot.

Blend the orange juice with the orange and lemon zest, soy sauce, honey and minced chiles, then pour over the chicken. Cover with the lid and cook on high for 3 to 5 hours. Drain off the cooking liquid into a small pan and bring to the boil. Blend the cornflour with 1 tablespoon of water, stir into the boiling sauce, and cook until thickened. Garnish the chicken with the herbs, and serve with the sauce and bread or new potatoes.

POT ROAST CHICKEN WITH CUCUMBER SAUCE

This is a variation on an old recipe that would have used boiling fowl, which today are difficult to find. However, using a roasting chicken instead reproduces the flavour just as well.

SERVES **4 to 6**   PREPARATION TIME **20 min**   COOKING TIME **Cook on high 4 to 5 hrs**

INGREDIENTS

1.3 kg (3 lb) whole chicken

1 lemon, preferably unwaxed or organic

Salt and fresh ground black pepper

1 tbsp sunflower oil

1 tbsp unsalted butter

1 shallot, peeled and chopped fine

1 small cucumber, peeled, seeded and diced

150 ml (5 fl oz) medium dry white wine

150 ml (5 fl oz) chicken stock

1 tbsp cornflour

4-5 tbsp double cream

Fresh herbs and cucumber, to garnish

Cooked vegetables, to serve

Preheat the slow cooker on high. Lightly rinse or wipe the chicken and dry with kitchen roll. Cut the lemon into small wedges, then season the cavity of the chicken and place the lemon wedges inside. Heat the oil and butter in a frying pan, then brown the chicken on all sides. Remove and place in the cooking pot and scatter over the shallot and cucumber. Heat the wine and stock to almost boiling, then pour over the chicken. Cover and cook on high for 4 to 5 hours or until tender.

Remove the chicken from the pot and keep warm while preparing the sauce. Pour 240 ml (8 fl oz) of the cooking liquid with the cucumber into a small pan and bring to the boil. Blend the cornflour with 1 tablespoon of water, then pour into the boiling liquid. Cook, stirring, until the mixture thickens. Stir in the cream and cook for 1 minute before adding seasoning to taste. Garnish the chicken and serve with the sauce and freshly cooked vegetables.

LEFT: *FLORIDA CHICKEN*

GUINEA HEN WITH ORANGE SAUCE

You can use poussin, pheasant or even chicken portions for this recipe. One pheasant will feed two people, and with poussin, you will probably need one each.

SERVES	4	PREPARATION TIME	15 min	COOKING TIME	Cook on high 3 to 4 hrs

INGREDIENTS

1 tbsp unsalted butter

1.3 kg (3 lb) oven-ready guinea hen, jointed

Salt and fresh ground black pepper

6 rashers bacon, chopped

2 tsp sunflower oil

2 shallots, peeled and chopped

2 tbsp plain flour

150 ml (5 fl oz) orange juice

150 ml (5 fl oz) white wine

1 tbsp soy sauce

2–3 tbsp orange marmalade

225 g (8 oz) peeled chestnuts

Fresh raspberries and herbs, to garnish

Preheat the slow cooker on high. Wipe the cooking pot with a little of the butter. Wipe or lightly rinse the guinea hen, pat dry and season. Melt the remaining butter in a frying pan and brown the guinea hen on all sides. Remove, drain and place in the cooking pot. Add the bacon to the frying pan and cook for 2 minutes.

Add the oil to the pan and sauté the shallots for 2 minutes, take off the heat and sprinkle in the flour. Cook for 2 minutes, then gradually stir in the orange juice, white wine, soy sauce, marmalade, chestnuts and seasoning. Cook, stirring, until the sauce comes to the boil, then pour over the guinea hen and cook for 3 to 4 hours. Skim off any excess fat. Serve the guinea hen with the sauce scattered with the raspberries and herbs.

TERIYAKI POUSSIN

When cooking poultry, with very few exceptions, it is important that the setting on your slow cooker is on high. This ensures that the poultry is cooked through thoroughly.

SERVES	4	PREPARATION TIME	5 min	COOKING TIME	Cook on high 3 to 5 hrs

INGREDIENTS

4 poussins, about 450 g (1 lb) each

Salt and fresh ground black pepper

225 g (8 oz) tinned pineapple chunks, reserving juice

Few sprigs fresh coriander

150 ml (5 fl oz) teriyaki sauce

2 tbsp honey

Fresh coriander sprigs and spring onion tassels, to garnish

Cooked white and wild rice, to serve

Preheat the slow cooker on high. Lightly rinse or wipe the poussins and season the cavities. Drain the pineapple, reserving the juice, and stuff the pineapple chunks into the poussin cavities together with a few sprigs of coriander. Place in the cooking pot.

Blend the tinned pineapple juice with the teriyaki sauce and honey, bring to the boil and pour over the poussins. Cover with a lid and cook on high for 3 to 5 hours. Remove from the pot and serve garnished with coriander sprigs and spring onion tassels and with the freshly cooked rice. For a thicker sauce, bring the liquid to the boil and stir in 1 tablespoon of cornflour blended with 2 tablespoons of water; cook, stirring, until thickened.

RIGHT: *GUINEA HEN WITH ORANGE SAUCE*

CHICKEN GUMBO SUPPER

This recipe is a complete meal in itself. You really do not need to add anything else, just the family or friends to sit and enjoy.

SERVES 6   PREPARATION TIME 15 min   COOKING TIME Cook on high 2 hrs then low 4 to 6 hrs

INGREDIENTS

450 g (1 lb) boned, skinned chicken thighs

4 thick garlic sausages such as Toulouse

1 tbsp olive oil

1 medium onion, peeled and chopped

2–4 garlic cloves, peeled and chopped

2 red serrano chiles, seeded and chopped

2 celery stalks, trimmed and sliced

2 large carrots, peeled and diced

410 g (14 ½ oz) tinned chopped tomatoes

240 ml (8 fl oz) chicken stock

Salt and fresh ground black pepper

1 tsp dried thyme

1 red pepper, seeded and chopped

225 g (8 oz) okra, trimmed and sliced thick

Hot pepper sauce, to taste

225 g (8 oz) cooked long-grain rice

Flat leaf parsley sprigs, to garnish

Cornbread and tossed green salad, to serve

Preheat the slow cooker on high. Cut the chicken thighs and sausages into bite-size pieces and place in the cooking pot. Add the remaining ingredients, except the red pepper, okra, hot pepper sauce and rice. Cover and cook on high for 2 hours then reduce the temperature to low and continue to cook for 3 hours.

Meanwhile, cover the red pepper with boiling water, drain and add to the cooker with the okra, hot pepper sauce and the cooked rice. Continue to cook for 1 to 3 hours until tender. Garnish and serve with cornbread, tossed green salad and extra hot pepper sauce.

TURKEY TAGINE

This recipe takes its inspiration from Morocco and, to continue with the theme, is served with couscous.

SERVES **4**   PREPARATION TIME **25 min**   COOKING TIME **Cook on high 3 to 5 hrs**

INGREDIENTS

450 g (1 lb) diced turkey meat

2 tbsp plain flour

Salt and fresh ground black pepper

2 tbsp sunflower oil

1 medium onion, peeled and cut into wedges

3–4 garlic cloves, peeled and sliced

1 tsp ground cumin

1 tsp ground coriander

1 cinnamon stick, lightly bashed

Large pinch of saffron

2 large carrots, peeled and sliced

300 ml (10 fl oz) turkey or chicken stock

75 g (2 ½ oz) chopped dried apricots

3 tomatoes, chopped

410 g (14 ½ oz) tinned chickpeas, drained

1 tbsp fresh coriander

Steamed couscous, to serve

Preheat the slow cooker on high. Trim and discard any sinew or fat from the meat, then toss in the flour seasoned with salt and pepper. Heat 1 tablespoon of the oil in a pan and gently sauté the onion and garlic for 3 minutes. With a slotted spoon, transfer to the cooking pot.

Add the remaining oil to the pan and sear the turkey meat on all sides. Sprinkle in the ground spices with the cinnamon stick and saffron, add the carrots and cook, stirring frequently, for 3 minutes. Add the stock, stirring throughout. Bring to the boil, add the apricots and tomatoes, then pour over the onions in the cooking pot and mix lightly.

Cover the cooking pot with the lid and cook for 2 hours. Add the drained chickpeas and continue to cook for another 1 to 3 hours. Remove the cinnamon stick, sprinkle with the coriander and serve with the freshly prepared couscous.

DUCK WITH CHERRIES

If using a frozen duck, ensure it is thoroughly thawed. If you are in a rush, submerge the duck, still in its wrappings, in cold water.

SERVES **4**   PREPARATION TIME **15 min**   COOKING TIME **Cook on high 4 to 5 hrs**

INGREDIENTS

1.8 kg (4 lb) oven-ready duck

1 small apple

1 small onion, peeled and cut into wedges

1 tbsp unsalted butter

410 g (14 ½ oz) tinned sour cherries

1 tbsp white wine or balsamic vinegar

1 tbsp arrowroot

Salt and fresh ground black pepper

100 g (3 ½ oz) peeled, skinned and rough chopped chestnuts

Fresh rocket, to garnish

Preheat the slow cooker on high. Discard any excess fat from inside the duck cavity and prick the skin with a fork. Rinse, and pat dry with kitchen roll. Core the apple, then cut into wedges and place along with the onion wedges in the duck cavity. Melt the butter in a frying pan and brown the duck on all sides, then place in the cooking pot and cover. Cook on high for 3 hours. Drain off and discard the fat.

Drain the tin of cherries into a measuring cup. Add water to the juice to make it up to 300 ml (10 fl oz) of liquid. Reserve the cherries. Pour the liquid into a small pan, stir in the vinegar and bring to the boil. Blend the arrowroot with 1 tablespoon of water, then stir into the boiling liquid. Cook, stirring, until the sauce thickens slightly. Add seasoning and the reserved cherries and chestnuts, then pour over the duck and continue to cook for 1 to 2 hours. Serve garnished with rocket.

CHICKEN RISOTTO

Normally when making a risotto you have to make sure that the risotto does not dry out. With the slow cooker this is not necessary.

SERVES **4 to 6**   PREPARATION TIME **15 minutes, plus soaking time**   COOKING TIME **Cook on high 3 to 5 hrs**

INGREDIENTS

1 tbsp dried mushrooms

1 tbsp unsalted butter

3 shallots, peeled and cut into thin wedges

2–4 garlic cloves, peeled and minced

¼–½ tsp saffron strands

1 tbsp grated lemon zest

350 g (12 oz) fresh skinless, boneless chicken, diced

225 g (8 oz) quick cooking risotto rice

300 ml (10 fl oz) white wine

600 ml (20 fl oz) chicken stock

75 g (2 ½ oz) sliced button mushrooms

3 tomatoes, seeded and chopped

75 g (2 ½ oz) peas, thawed if frozen

Salt and fresh ground black pepper

2 tbsp chopped fresh chervil or parsley

Lemon wedges, to garnish

Fresh shaved Parmesan, to serve

Preheat the cooker on high. Soak the dried mushrooms in almost boiling water for 20 minutes, then drain, reserving the soaking liquid. Heat the butter in a large frying pan; when melted, sauté the shallots and garlic for 2 minutes before sprinkling in the saffron strands, lemon zest and chicken. Cook, stirring, until the chicken is seared, then sprinkle in the rice and cook for 2 more minutes. Stir frequently. Pour in the wine and 475 ml (16 fl oz) of the stock, then strain the mushroom soaking liquid into the pan together with the soaked mushrooms, button mushrooms and tomatoes. Bring to the boil and spoon into the cooking pot. Cover with the lid and cook on high for 2 hours.

Add the peas and remaining stock if necessary, and continue to cook for 1 to 3 hours. Adjust the seasoning to taste, stir in the chopped herbs and serve garnished with the lemon wedges and the Parmesan cheese.

LEFT: *DUCK WITH CHERRIES*

CHINESE STYLE DUCK

This is the nearest that you can get to a stir-fry in your slow cooker. Reducing the temperature to low after 1 hour keeps the vegetables reasonably crisp.

SERVES **4**   PREPARATION TIME **15 min**   COOKING TIME **Cook on high 1 hr then low 3 to 4 hrs**

INGREDIENTS

1 tbsp dried Chinese mushrooms

450 g (1 lb) duck breast with fat removed

1 large carrot, peeled

2 celery stalks, trimmed

225 g (8 oz) tinned pineapple chunks

100 g (3 ½ oz) lychees, peeled and stoned if fresh

1 tbsp sunflower oil

1 red onion, peeled and cut into wedges

100 g (3 ½ oz) water chestnuts

1 tbsp hoisin sauce

2 tbsp light soy sauce

2 tbsp cornflour

4 spring onions, trimmed and shredded, to garnish

Cooked rice, to serve

Preheat the slow cooker on high while preparing ingredients. Soak the mushrooms in almost boiling water for 20 minutes. Drain, reserving the liquid and mushrooms. Slice the mushrooms if large. Cut the duck breasts into thin strips, set aside, then cut the carrot and celery into matchsticks. Drain the pineapple, reserving the juice and flesh, and cut the lychees in half.

Heat the oil in a frying pan and sauté the duck breasts until sealed. Using a slotted spoon, transfer to the slow cooker cooking pot. Add the onion, carrots and celery to the pan and cook for 2 minutes, stirring frequently. Then add the drained mushrooms and water chestnuts.

Blend the hoisin and soy sauce together and add to the pan. Blend the cornflour with the pineapple juice, stir in the reserved mushroom liquid, pour into the pan and bring to the boil. Cook, stirring, until thickened, then pour over the duck, cover and cook for 1 hour. Reduce the temperature, add the pineapple and lychees, and continue to cook for 3 to 4 hours. Serve sprinkled with spring onions and with the freshly cooked fried rice.

CHICKEN WITH 40 GARLIC CLOVES

The fragrant aroma that comes from the kitchen while this dish is cooking is wonderful. Serve with plenty of rice and ratatouille.

SERVES **4 to 6**   PREPARATION TIME **10 min**   COOKING TIME **Cook on high 3 to 5 hrs**

INGREDIENTS

50 g (1 ¾ oz) unsalted butter

1.3 kg (3 lb) oven-ready chicken

Salt and fresh ground black pepper

40 whole unpeeled garlic cloves

Fresh herbs, to garnish

Cooked rice and ratatouille, to serve

Preheat the slow cooker on high and wipe the cooking pot with a little of the butter. Wipe or lightly rinse the chicken and pat dry with kitchen roll then season and stuff the cavity with about half the garlic cloves.

Melt half of the butter in a frying pan and brown the chicken all over. Remove and place in the cooking pot, then scatter over the remaining unpeeled garlic cloves. Melt the remaining butter and pour over the chicken, cover and cook on high for 3 to 5 hours. Serve the chicken with the garlic, garnished with herbs and accompanied by the rice and ratatouille.

RIGHT: *CHINESE STYLE DUCK*

TURKEY WITH WINE AND PEPPERS

Although this is a casserole style dish, it would be ideal to serve for either a formal or family occasion. Simply vary the accompaniments.

SERVES **4**   PREPARATION TIME **15 min**   COOKING TIME **Cook on high 3 to 5 hrs**

INGREDIENTS

675 g (1 ½ lb) turkey breast

2 tbsp plain flour

Salt and fresh ground black pepper

2 tbsp sunflower oil

1 large white onion, peeled and cut into wedges

3–4 garlic cloves, peeled and minced

6 bacon rashers, chopped

1 red pepper, seeded and sliced

1 yellow pepper, seeded and sliced

3 tbsp brandy

240 ml (8 fl oz) red wine

120 ml (4 fl oz) turkey or chicken stock

Fresh rocket leaves, to garnish

Creamed potatoes, salad and crusty bread, to serve

Preheat the slow cooker on high while preparing the ingredients. Trim the turkey of any sinew or fat, then cut into bite-size pieces. Season the flour with salt and pepper, then toss over the turkey, reserving any remaining flour.

Heat 1 tablespoon of the oil in a large pan and sauté the turkey until seared all over, remove from the pan, and set aside. Add the remaining oil to the pan and sauté the onion, garlic and bacon for 3 minutes. Add the peppers and any remaining flour to the pan and continue to cook, stirring, for 1 minute. Return the turkey to the pan, add the brandy and heat for 1 minute. Take the pan off the heat and ignite. When all the flames have subsided, gradually stir in the wine and stock. Return to the heat and cook, stirring, until the mixture comes to the boil. Carefully pour into the cooking pot.

Cover and cook on high for 3 to 5 hours. Adjust the seasoning. Serve garnished with rocket leaves and accompanied by the potatoes, salad and crusty bread to mop up all the juices.

DUCK
JAMBALAYA

Jambalaya was created in the 18th century and is a cajun/creole dish. It normally contains pork, usually in the form of chorizo. However, there are no rules, so add what strikes your fancy.

SERVES 4 to 6   **PREPARATION TIME** 20 min   **COOKING TIME** Cook on high 2 to 4 hrs

INGREDIENTS

3 boneless duck breasts

4 slices smoked fatty bacon, chopped

1 white onion, peeled and chopped

2-4 garlic cloves, peeled and minced

2 celery sticks, trimmed and chopped

1 green pepper, seeded and chopped

410 g (14 ½ oz) tinned chopped tomatoes

Hot pepper sauce, to taste

Pinch cayenne pepper

Fresh ground black pepper

175 g (6 oz) quick cooking brown rice

50 g (1 ¾ oz) wild rice

225 g (8 oz) chorizo, or other spicy sausage, cut into chunks

1 tsp dried thyme

2-3 tsp Worcester sauce

900 ml (30 fl oz) chicken stock

Diagonally sliced spring onions, to garnish

Crusty bread, to serve

Preheat the cooker on high while preparing the ingredients. Remove the fat from the duck breasts and cut into slices. Place the bacon into a nonstick frying pan and cook gently until the fat begins to run out. Add the duck pieces and brown all over, then remove and reserve.

Add the onion, garlic, celery and green pepper to the pan and cook gently for 3 minutes, stirring frequently. Return the duck to the pan, then add all the other ingredients except the spring onions. Bring to the boil and pour into the cooking pot. Cover with the lid and cook on high for 2 to 4 hours. Adjust the seasoning, sprinkle with sliced spring onions and serve with crusty bread.

TURKEY MOLE

You can serve this either as a filling for tacos or burritos or accompanied by cornbread, rice, guacamole or sour cream.

SERVES **4 to 6**   PREPARATION TIME **30 min**   COOKING TIME **Cook on high 3 to 5 hrs**

INGREDIENTS

6 dried pasilla chilis

20 whole blanched almonds

2 tbsp pine nuts

Small cinnamon stick

3 whole cloves

1 onion, peeled and sliced

2 garlic cloves, peeled and minced

2 ½ tbsp toasted sesame seeds

1 tsp ground coriander

Fresh ground black pepper

2 tbsp sunflower oil

300 ml (10 fl oz) chicken stock

410 g (14 ½ oz) tinned chopped tomatoes

2 squares (50 g/1 ¾ oz) plain chocolate

450 g (1 lb) boneless, skinless turkey thighs, diced

Sesame seeds, spring onions, to garnish

Tomato and red onion salad, to serve

Preheat the cooker on high, 20 minutes before cooking. Rehydrate the dried chilis in almost boiling water and leave for at least 20 minutes, longer if time permits. Drain the chilis and place in a food processor with the almonds, pine nuts, cinnamon, cloves, onion, garlic, sesame seeds, ground coriander and black pepper and blend to form a paste. Heat 1 tablespoon of the oil in a frying pan and fry the paste for 5 minutes. Stir frequently. Add the stock and tomatoes, then simmer for 10 minutes. Add the chocolate and cook until the chocolate has melted. Remove from the heat and reserve.

Meanwhile, heat the remaining oil in a large pan and sear the turkey on all sides. Add to the reserved sauce then spoon into the cooking pot. Cook for 3 to 5 hours. Serve sprinkled with extra sesame seeds, sliced spring onions and a tomato and red onion salad.

CHICKEN WITH PASTA

Try adding toasted pine nuts, lemon zest and mint – or chopped dried apricots, fresh coriander and orange zest with a few chopped pecans.

SERVES **4**   PREPARATION TIME **10 min**   COOKING TIME **Cook on high 1 hr then low 4 to 5 hrs**

INGREDIENTS

450 g (1 lb) chicken mince

6 spring onions, trimmed and chopped fine

2 garlic cloves, peeled and minced

4 sundried tomatoes, drained if in oil and chopped fine

1 tbsp tomato purée

Salt and fresh ground black pepper

1 tsp dried oregano

50 g (1 ¾ oz) fresh brown bread crumbs

1 large egg, beaten

410 g (14 ½ oz) tinned chopped tomatoes

1 small onion, peeled and grated

2 tsp Worcester sauce

Fresh oregano sprigs, to garnish

Cooked pasta, grated Parmesan, warm Italian style bread and tossed bitter leaf salad, to serve

Preheat the slow cooker on high. Mix together the chicken mince, spring onions, garlic, sundried tomatoes, tomato purée, seasoning and the dried oregano. Add the bread crumbs, then bind together with the beaten egg. Shape into small meatballs and place in the slow cooker cooking pot.

Blend the chopped tomatoes and their juice with the grated onion, Worcester sauce and seasoning, then pour over the meatballs.
Cover and cook on high for 1 hour, then reduce the heat to low and cook for 4 to 5 hours. Skim off any excess oil. Serve on the freshly cooked pasta with grated Parmesan cheese and oregano sprigs, accompanied by warm bread and tossed salad.

LEFT: *Turkey Mole*

VEGETABLES

Slow cookers are mostly associated with meat stews and casseroles. However, with or without meat, it is equally possible to produce delicious meals to captivate even the most discerning meat eater or vegetarian.

MUSHROOM MEDLEY

If you prefer a thicker sauce, at the end of the cooking time pour the liquid into a small pan, blend 1 tablespoon of cornflour with 2 tablespoons of water, stir into the cooking liquid and bring to the boil. Cook, stirring until thickened.

SERVES **4**   PREPARATION TIME **15 mins, plus 20 mins soaking**   COOKING TIME **Cook on high 3 to 4 hrs**   AUTO COOK **4 to 6 hrs**

INGREDIENTS

15 g (½ oz) dried mushrooms

1 tbsp olive oil

4 shallots, peeled and cut into wedges

2–3 garlic cloves, peeled and minced

1–2 red jalapeño chiles, seeded and chopped

300 g (10 oz) baby potatoes, diced

1 tbsp balsamic vinegar

150 ml (5 fl oz) white wine

450 g (1 lb) assorted mushrooms, wiped and sliced if large

4 plum tomatoes, peeled, seeded and chopped

1–2 tbsp chopped fresh basil, to garnish

Freshly shaved Parmesan cheese and warm crusty bread, to serve

LEFT: *Warm Bean and Pumpkin Salad (page 108)*

Rinse the dried mushrooms in cold water, place in a small bowl and cover with almost boiling water and leave for 20 minutes. Drain, strain the soaking liquid, and reserve. Slice any of the soaked mushrooms if large.

Preheat the cooker on high. Heat the oil in a frying pan and sauté the shallots, garlic, and chiles for 3 minutes. Add the potatoes and sauté for 2 more minutes, then place in the cooking pot with all the mushrooms and the tomatoes. Heat the soaking liquid and white wine until almost boiling, then add the vinegar and pour over the mushrooms. Cover and cook on high for 3 to 4 hours. Sprinkle over the chopped basil and shaved Parmesan cheese and serve with the warm crusty bread. (This dish is also delicious served cold.)

PEPPER AND RED KIDNEY BEAN RICE

Quick cooking brown rice stands up best of all to the long slow cooking. If cooking for vegetarians, substitute 1 tsp concentrated vegetable bouillon for the thai fish sauce.

SERVES **4 to 6**   PREPARATION TIME **10 min, plus 20 mins soaking**   COOKING TIME **Cook on high 4 to 5 hrs**   AUTO COOK **6 to 8 hrs**

INGREDIENTS

1 tbsp dried shiitake mushrooms

1 tbsp peanut oil

4 shallots, peeled and cut into wedges

2–4 garlic cloves, peeled and chopped

1–2 Thai chiles, seeded and chopped

175 g (6 oz) quick cooking brown rice, rinsed

1 lemon grass stalk, outer leaves discarded, chopped

2 kaffir lime leaves, crumbled if dried

2 small red peppers, seeded and chopped

600 ml (20 fl oz) vegetable stock

1 tbsp light soy sauce

2 tsp Thai fish sauce

1 tsp honey

200 g (7 oz) tinned red kidney beans, drained and rinsed

225 g (8 oz) sliced button mushrooms

1 tbsp chopped fresh coriander

Preheat the slow cooker on high while preparing the ingredients. Soak the dried mushrooms in almost boiling water for 20 minutes, drain, reserving the liquid. Heat the oil in a pan and sauté the shallots, garlic and chiles for 3 minutes. Add the rice, lemon grass, kaffir lime leaves, red pepper, stock, soy and fish sauces, reserved soaked mushrooms and their liquid and honey. Bring to the boil. Pour into the cooking pot and cook for 3 hours.

Add the kidney beans and button mushrooms and continue to cook for 1 to 2 hours. Sprinkle with coriander and serve.

ORANGE-GLAZED CARROTS

This is very quick to throw together, and the result is a really interesting and different way of enjoying carrots.

SERVES **6**   PREPARATION TIME **5 min**   COOKING TIME **Cook on low 6 to 8 hrs**

INGREDIENTS

900 g (2 lb) baby carrots

120 ml (4 fl oz) freshly squeezed orange juice

Grated zest of 2 oranges

2 tbsp butter

60 ml (2 fl oz) honey

Salt and freshly ground black pepper, to taste

Freshly chopped parsley, to serve

Put all the ingredients except for the parsley in the slow cooker, cover and cook on low for 6-8 hours, or until the carrots are tender.

Serve sprinkled with freshly chopped parsley.

TUSCAN BEAN STEW

When using dried beans it is important that they are soaked overnight in water. Red kidney beans should be boiled vigorously for 10 minutes, drained, rinsed and used as directed.

SERVES **4 to 6**   PREPARATION TIME **10 mins, plus overnight soaking**   COOKING TIME **Cook on low 8 to 10 hrs**   AUTO COOK **12 to 14 hrs**

INGREDIENTS

175 g (6 oz) dried red kidney beans

175 g (6 oz) dried cranberry beans

1 tbsp olive oil

1 red onion, peeled and cut into wedges

2-4 garlic cloves, peeled and chopped

1 small red jalapeño chile, seeded and chopped

1 Florence fennel bulb, trimmed and cut into wedges

1 yellow pepper, seeded and chopped

450 g (1 lb) chopped plum tomatoes

2 tbsp tomato purée

Salt and fresh ground black pepper

1 tsp dried oregano

300 ml (10 fl oz) vegetable stock

1 large courgette

2 tbsp chopped fresh parsley, to garnish

Warm crusty bread, sour cream and salad, to serve

Cover the dried beans with cold water and leave to soak overnight. Next day, drain the beans, place in a pan and cover with water. Bring to the boil and boil for 10 minutes, drain and set aside.

Preheat the slow cooker on high while preparing ingredients. Heat the oil in a frying pan and sauté the onion, garlic and chile for 3 minutes. Place in the cooking pot of the slow cooker, add the beans and all the remaining ingredients except for the courgette, and stir well. Cover, reduce the heat and cook for 7 ½ hours.

Meanwhile, trim the courgette and dice small. Cover with boiling water, then drain and add to the cooking pot 30 minutes before the end of the cooking time. Stir well, then continue to cook for another 30 minutes to 2 hours. Sprinkle with the parsley and serve with crusty bread, sour cream and salad.

LEFT: *Orange-Glazed Carrots*

STUFFED PEPPERS

These stuffed peppers proved a great success. The stuffing is so good and versatile that it can be used to stuff aubergine and courgettes too.

| SERVES | 4 | PREPARATION TIME | 15 min | COOKING TIME | Cook on high 2 to 4 hrs |

INGREDIENTS

4 assorted coloured peppers

75 g (2 ½ oz) instant couscous

6 spring onions, trimmed and chopped

50 g (1 ¾ oz) raisins

1 tbsp grated lemon zest

¼–1 tsp dried minced chiles, according to taste

2 tomatoes, seeded and chopped

50 g (1 ¾ oz) strong flavoured cheese, such as Cheddar, grated

2 tbsp toasted pine nuts

1 tbsp chopped fresh flat-leaf parsley

Salt and fresh ground black pepper

1 extra large egg, beaten

150 ml (5 fl oz) vegetable stock

Flat-leaf parsley, to garnish

Preheat the slow cooker on high. Cut the peppers either in half lengthwise. Remove and discard the seeds and membrane, then cover with boiling water and leave for 5 minutes, then drain and set aside. Meanwhile place the couscous in a bowl, cover with boiling water and leave until all the water has been absorbed. Add ⅔ of the chopped spring onions, the raisins, lemon zest, chiles, tomatoes, cheese, pine nuts, parsley and seasoning to taste. Mix well, then bind together with the beaten egg. Use to stuff the peppers, then place in the cooking pot. Heat the stock and pour around the peppers, cover with the lid and cook on high for 2 to 4 hours. Serve garnished with flat-leaf parsley and the remaining spring onions.

COURGETTES WITH APPLE AND FILBERT STUFFING

This stuffing could be used to stuff any vegetables, but it is great with squash. For a change, serve it with a fresh tangy tomato sauce.

| SERVES | 4 | PREPARATION TIME | 15 min | COOKING TIME | Cook on low 4 to 6 hrs |

INGREDIENTS

4 medium-size courgettes

1 tbsp butter

2 shallots, peeled and chopped

2–3 garlic cloves, peeled and minced

1 medium apple, peeled and grated

50 g (1 ¾ oz) chopped filberts

50 g (1 ¾ oz) soft bread crumbs

75 g (2 ½ oz) strong flavoured grated cheese such as Swiss or Cheddar

Salt and fresh ground black pepper

1 tsp dried sage

2 large eggs, beaten

150 ml (5 fl oz) apple juice

Apple sauce, to serve

Apple slices and fresh sage, to garnish

Preheat the cooker on high. Peel the courgettes, cut in half lengthwise and scoop out the centres. Heat the butter in a small pan and sauté the shallots and garlic for 2 minutes, remove from the heat and stir in the apple, filberts, bread crumbs, two-thirds of the cheese, seasoning and the sage. Mix to a stiff consistency with the egg. Use to stuff the courgettes.

Place the stuffed vegetables in the cooking pot, sprinkle with the remaining cheese and pour around the apple juice. Cook on low for 4 to 6 hours. Serve with the apple sauce, garnished with the apple slices and fresh sage. If preferred, place the cooked courgettes under a preheated grill, sprinkle the tops with a little extra cheese and grill to brown the top.

RIGHT: *STUFFED PEPPERS*

WARM BEAN AND PUMPKIN SALAD

The spinach cooks so quickly that it is added right at the very end of the cooking time. You could use frozen spinach, but fresh is definitely better. For a change, use chard in place of the spinach.

| SERVES | 6 | PREPARATION TIME | 30 min plus overnight soaking | COOKING TIME | Cook on high 8 to 10 hrs | AUTO COOK | 10 to 12 hrs |

INGREDIENTS

100 g (3 ½ oz) dried haricot beans, soaked overnight

100 g (3 ½ oz) dried red kidney beans, soaked overnight

100 g (3 ½ oz) dried black eye peas, soaked overnight

2 tbsp olive oil

1 large onion, peeled and cut into wedges

Small piece fresh ginger, peeled and grated

2–4 garlic cloves, peeled and chopped

¼–1 tsp dried minced chiles

1 tsp cumin seeds

1 tsp ground coriander

½ tsp turmeric

450 g (1 lb) pumpkin, peeled, seeded and diced

300 ml (10 fl oz) vegetable stock

100 g (3 ½ oz) cherry tomatoes, quartered

175 g (6 oz) spinach, thoroughly washed and shredded

175 g (6 oz) feta cheese, diced

Fresh coriander sprigs

Salt and fresh ground black pepper

Sour cream or reduced-fat plain yoghurt and warm pita bread strips, to serve

Cover the beans and peas with cold water and leave to soak overnight. Next day, drain, place in a pan and cover with water. Bring to the boil and boil for 10 minutes. Drain and reserve.

Preheat the slow cooker on high. Heat the oil in a frying pan and sauté the onion with the ginger, garlic, chiles to taste and all the spices for 3 minutes. Add the pumpkin and continue to sauté for 3 more minutes, then spoon into the cooking pot and stir in the drained beans. Heat the stock to boiling and pour over the vegetables and beans. Cover, reduce temperature to low, then cook for 8 to 10 hours.

Just before serving, stir in the tomatoes and spinach, stir well and continue to cook for 15 to 20 minutes or until the spinach has begun to wilt. Sprinkle with the diced feta cheese and the freshly chopped coriander and serve with sour cream or yoghurt and strips of warm pita bread.

MOROCCAN HOT POT

Frying the spices before cooking in the cooking pot intensifies their flavour. It is important to use your spices quickly as they can lose their aroma – buy in small quantities and store in a cool dark place.

SERVES **6**   PREPARATION TIME **15 min**   COOKING TIME **Cook on low 4 to 6 hrs**   AUTO COOK **6 to 8 hrs**

INGREDIENTS

1 tbsp olive oil

1 onion, peeled and cut into wedges

2–4 garlic cloves, peeled and chopped

1 red jalapeño chile, seeded and chopped

1 tsp cumin seeds

1 tsp ground coriander

¼–½ tsp saffron or turmeric

2 medium carrots

350 g (12 oz) baby aubergines, trimmed and halved or quartered if large

300 g (10 oz) diced squash

1 cinnamon stick, bruised

410 g (14 ½ oz) tinned chopped tomatoes

150 ml (5 fl oz) vegetable stock

50 g (1 ¾ oz) stoned prunes, chopped

Salt and fresh ground black pepper

410 g (14 ½ oz) tinned chickpeas, drained

4 baby courgettes, trimmed, halved and blanched

Freshly prepared couscous, to serve

Preheat the slow cooker while preparing the ingredients. Heat the oil in a frying pan and sauté the onion, garlic, chile and spices for 3 minutes, stirring frequently. Add the remaining vegetables and bruised cinnamon stick and place in the cooking pot.

Heat the chopped tomatoes with the stock, add the prunes, seasoning and chickpeas, then pour over the vegetables in the pot and cover. Reduce the heat to low and cook for 3 ½ hours. Add the blanched, halved courgettes and cook for a further 30 minutes to 2 hours. Serve with the freshly prepared couscous.

RATATOUILLE WITH KIDNEY BEANS

This recipe uses tinned red kidney beans. You can use dried, but remember to boil for 10 minutes and go easy on the seasoning as too much salt can toughen beans.

SERVES **4**   PREPARATION TIME **15 min**   COOKING TIME **Cook on high 4 to 5 hrs**   AUTO COOK **5 to 8 hrs**

INGREDIENTS

1 tbsp olive oil

1 large onion, peeled and chopped

2–4 garlic cloves, peeled and chopped

1 large aubergine, trimmed and diced

450 g (1 lb) chopped ripe plum tomatoes

1 red pepper, seeded and chopped

1 yellow pepper, seeded and chopped

410 g (14 ½ oz) tinned red kidney beans, drained and rinsed

150 ml (5 fl oz) red wine or vegetable stock

Salt and fresh ground black pepper

175 g (6 oz) sliced button mushrooms

2 courgettes, trimmed and sliced

2 tbsp chopped fresh basil

Fresh basil sprigs, to garnish

Freshly shaved Parmesan cheese and warm crusty bread, to serve

Preheat the slow cooker on high. Heat the oil in a frying pan and sauté the onion, garlic and aubergine for 5 minutes. Add all the remaining ingredients except for the mushrooms, courgettes and 1 tablespoon of the chopped basil and stir well. Spoon into the cooking pot and cover with the lid.

Cook on high for 3 hours, then add the mushrooms and courgettes and continue to cook for 1 to 3 more hours. Garnish with the fresh basil sprigs, the remaining chopped basil and the freshly shaved Parmesan cheese. Serve with crusty bread.

BARBECUED BEANS

You can replace the treacle with maple syrup. The treacle gives a hearty flavour, while the maple syrup gives the beans a more delicate flavour.

SERVES **4 to 6**   PREPARATION TIME **15 min plus overnight soaking**   COOKING TIME **Cook on low 8 to 10 hrs**   AUTO COOK **10 to 14 hrs**

INGREDIENTS

225 g (8 oz) dried haricot beans, soaked overnight

1 large onion, peeled and chopped

2–4 garlic cloves, peeled and minced

6 tbsp tomato ketchup

1 tbsp treacle

1 tbsp brown sugar

1 tsp ready-made grainy or English mustard

240 ml (8 fl oz) vegetable stock

Coriander sprigs, to garnish

Warm bread, to serve

Cover the beans with cold water, cover and leave overnight. Next day, preheat the cooker on high. Drain the beans, place in a pan, cover with water and bring to the boil. Boil gently for 10 minutes, then drain and place in the cooking pot. Add the chopped onion with the garlic and stir well. Blend the tomato ketchup with the treacle, sugar, mustard and stock. Pour over the beans and stir well. Cover, reduce the temperature to low and cook for 8 to 10 hours. Serve, garnished with coriander sprigs and wedges of warm bread, coleslaw and tomato salad.

STUFFED ACORN SQUASH

These lovely squash are cooked in orange juice, which gives them a fruity flavour. This is a perfect dish for a vegetarian.

SERVES **4**   PREPARATION TIME **15 min**   COOKING TIME **Cook on high 3 to 4 hrs**   AUTO COOK **4 to 6 hrs**

INGREDIENTS

2 large or 4 small acorn squash

1 yellow pepper, seeded and chopped fine

3 shallots, peeled and chopped fine

410 g (14 ½ oz) tinned hearts of palm, drained, rinsed and chopped

3 medium tomatoes, seeded and chopped

200 g (7 oz) tinned chickpeas, drained and rinsed

1 red apple, cored and chopped

1 tbsp maple syrup or clear honey

Salt and fresh ground black pepper

240 ml (8 fl oz) orange juice

2 tbsp cashews, chopped

2 tbsp finely shredded fresh mint

Preheat the cooker on high while preparing ingredients. Cut the squash in half and scoop out and discard the seeds. Mix all the remaining ingredients together except for the orange juice, the cashew nuts and 1 tablespoon of the shredded mint.

Spoon into the squash halves and place in the cooking pot. Pour around the orange juice. Cover and cook on high for 3 to 4 hours. Serve sprinkled with the cashews and the remaining mint.

Left: *Barbecued Beans*

SPICY VEGETABLES WITH COCONUT

Vary the vegetables according to personal taste and availability. There is a growing demand for organic vegetables as they taste better and have not been sprayed or treated with pesticides.

SERVES **4 to 6**   PREPARATION TIME **20 min**   COOKING TIME **Cook on high 3 to 4 hrs or low 5 to 8 hrs**   AUTO COOK **8 to 10 hrs**

INGREDIENTS

2 tbsp sunflower oil

1 white onion, peeled and cut into wedges

2–4 garlic cloves, peeled and chopped

1–3 red serrano chiles, seeded and chopped

Small piece ginger, peeled and grated

1 tsp ground coriander

1 tsp turmeric

1 sweet potato, peeled and diced

1 small head cauliflower, divided into florets

2 carrots, peeled and sliced

1 red pepper, seeded and chopped

4 tomatoes, peeled if preferred, seeded and chopped

2 tbsp ground blanched almonds

150 ml (5 fl oz) vegetable stock

240 ml (8 fl oz) coconut milk

Salt and fresh ground black pepper

Wheat wraps, to serve

Preheat the cooker on high while preparing the ingredients. Heat the oil in a frying pan and sauté the onion, garlic, chiles and ginger for 2 minutes. Add the spices and continue to sauté for another 3 minutes. Add all the prepared vegetables, then blend the ground almonds with the stock and coconut milk and bring almost to boiling point, stirring throughout.

Spoon or pour into the cooking pot and add a little seasoning. Stir, cover and cook on high for 3 to 5 hours, or on low for 5 to 8 hours. Adjust seasoning and serve with the wheat wraps.

WINTER VEGETABLE CASSEROLE

The beauty of French lentils, unlike other lentils, is that they keep their shape throughout the cooking process. Many people regard them as the best flavoured, too.

SERVES 4 to 6   **PREPARATION TIME** 10 min   **COOKING TIME** Cook on high 3 to 4 hrs   **AUTO COOK** 4 to 7 hrs

INGREDIENTS

1 tbsp sunflower oil

1 onion, peeled and cut into wedges

2–3 garlic cloves, peeled and chopped

1–2 red serrano chiles, seeded and chopped

1 tsp fennel seeds

½ tsp caraway seeds

2 medium carrots, peeled and sliced

1 acorn squash, peeled, seeded and diced

175 g (6 oz) French lentils, rinsed

300 g (10 oz) diced turnip

1 Florence fennel bulb, trimmed and sliced

750 ml (25 fl oz) vegetable stock

1 tsp dried mixed herbs

Few dashes Tabasco or hot sauce, to taste

Salt and fresh ground black pepper

2 tbsp chopped fresh parsley, to garnish

Goats' cheese, crumbled, to serve

Preheat the cooker on high. Heat the oil in a frying pan and sauté the onion, garlic, chiles and fennel and caraway seeds for 3 minutes. Place in the cooking pot and add the rest of the ingredients except for the chopped parsley and cheese. Mix well.

Cook on high for 3 to 4 hours. Serve sprinkled with the chopped parsley and crumbled goats' cheese.

THREE BEAN LASAGNE

Use pre-cooked lasagne sheets, breaking them to fit the cooking pot. Although this recipe uses beans, you can cook your favourite meat lasagne recipe in exactly the same way.

SERVES	4 to 6	PREPARATION TIME	10 min	COOKING TIME	Cook on low 4 to 5 hrs	AUTO COOK	5 to 7 hrs

INGREDIENTS

1 tsp butter

1 tbsp oil

1 onion, peeled and chopped

2 garlic cloves, peeled and minced

410 g (14 ½ oz) tinned borlotti beans, drained and rinsed

300 g (10 oz) tinned cannellini beans, drained and rinsed

225 g (8 oz) broad beans, thawed if frozen

410 g (14 ½ oz) tinned chopped tomatoes

1 tsp dried oregano

Salt and fresh ground black pepper

8–12 sheets no-boil lasagne

600 ml (20 fl oz) prepared béchamel sauce

50 g (1 ¾ oz) freshly grated Parmesan cheese

Warm Italian bread; tossed green salad and tomato, black olive and basil salad, to serve

Preheat the slow cooker on high. Lightly grease the inside of the cooking pot with the butter. Heat the oil in a frying pan, then sauté the onion and garlic for 3 minutes. Add all the drained beans, the chopped tomatoes, dried oregano and the seasoning, and mix well.

Arrange a layer of the bean mixture in the base of the cooking pot and cover with 2–3 lasagne sheets, breaking them to fit. Spoon over sufficient béchamel sauce to cover and sprinkle with a little of the grated Parmesan.

Continue layering, ending with a layer of cheese. Cover with the lid, reduce the cooker temperature to low and cook for 4 to 5 hours. Serve with plenty of warm Italian bread, a tossed green salad and a tomato and black olive with basil salad.

SLOW COOKED RED CABBAGE

Red cabbage is a wonderful vegetable, requiring long, slow cooking – ideal for the slow cooker. Once you've tried this recipe, you will never cook red cabbage any other way.

SERVES	4 to 6	PREPARATION TIME	10 min	COOKING TIME	Cook on low 4 to 5 hrs	AUTO COOK	5 to 7 hrs

INGREDIENTS

1 red cabbage, about 900 g (2 lb)

2 tbsp dark raw sugar

1 large sour apple, peeled, cored and chopped

2 tbsp red wine vinegar

Salt and fresh ground black pepper

½–1 tsp caraway seeds

240 ml (8 fl oz) water

Sour cream, to serve

Preheat the cooker on high while preparing the ingredients. Cut the cabbage into quarters and discard the tough outer leaves and the central core. Finely shred the cabbage, then wash thoroughly in plenty of cold water until the water runs clear. Place in the cooking pot. Add the remaining ingredients except the sour cream. Stir, then cover and cook on low for 4 to 5 hours. Stir again, then serve with the sour cream.

RIGHT: *THREE BEAN LASAGNE*

DESSERTS

Steamed puddings will always be an obvious choice for your slow cooker, but other desserts, fruit crumbles, cakes and even brownies are delicious when made in a slow cooker.

BLUEBERRY MUFFIN BAKE

As with conventional style muffins it is important that you do not overmix the ingredients, otherwise the finished bake will not be as light as it should be.

SERVES 6   PREPARATION TIME **10 min**   COOKING TIME **Cook on high 3 to 4 hrs**

INGREDIENTS

75 g (2 ½ oz) unsalted butter

75 g (2 ½ oz) light muscovado sugar

100 g (3 ½ oz) wholemeal self-raising flour

100 g (3 ½ oz) white self-raising flour; if substituting with plain flour, add 3 tsp baking powder and ½ tsp salt

1 tsp ground cinnamon

175 g (6 oz) fresh blueberries

50 g (1 ¾ oz) pecans, chopped

2 eggs, beaten

6–8 tbsp buttermilk

1–2 tsp demerara sugar

Cream or mascarpone cheese, to serve

Preheat the cooker on high. Lightly butter a 1.2-litre (2-pint) heatproof dish that will sit in the cooking pot, then place the remaining butter in a pan with the sugar and heat until melted. Sieve the flours and ground cinnamon into a mixing bowl, then stir in the bran left in the sieve from the wholemeal flour. Add the melted butter mixture and stir until blended. Add the blueberries and pecans, stir, then beat in the egg and sufficient buttermilk to give a soft dropping consistency. Take care not to overmix.

Spoon into the buttered dish, sprinkle the top with the light muscovado sugar, and place in the cooking pot. Pour around sufficient water to come halfway up the sides of the dish. Cover and cook on high for 3 to 4 hours. Serve with cream or mascarpone cheese.

LEFT: *CHOCOLATE FONDUE (PAGE 143)*

PEACH AND ALMOND CRISP

Crisps are always a family favourite, and one of the best ways of eating them is with plenty of cream and vanilla ice cream – how naughty is that? But how delicious! Try it when you are feeling really decadent.

SERVES	**4 to 6**	PREPARATION TIME	**10 min**	COOKING TIME	**Cook on high 4 to 5 hrs**	AUTO COOK	**5 to 7 hrs**

INGREDIENTS

1 tsp unsalted butter

6 ripe fresh peaches, skinned, stoned and sliced, or use tinned sliced peaches

5 tbsp peach or orange juice, optional

1 tbsp honey, optional

½ tsp almond extract

100 g (3 ½ oz) whole-wheat flour

50 g (1 ¾ oz) quick cooking oats

25 g (1 oz) ground blanched almonds

50 g (1 ¾ oz) raw sugar

1 tsp ground cinnamon

8 tbsp peanut butter

2 tbsp toasted slivered almonds

1 tsp caster sugar

Mint sprigs, to garnish

Cream, ice cream or frozen yoghurt, to serve

Preheat the cooker on high. Lightly grease a 1.2-litre (2-pint) heatproof dish with the butter, then either arrange the sliced fresh peaches in the base or drain the tinned peaches, reserving 4 tablespoons of their juice, and place the tinned peaches in the base.

If using fresh peaches, pour over the peach or orange juice and honey. If using tinned fruit, use the tinned juice. Sprinkle the fresh or tinned peaches with the almond essence.

Place the flour, oats, almonds, sugar and cinnamon into a bowl, add the peanut butter, and blend in. Sprinkle over the peaches and pat down lightly. Cover with the lid, then reduce the temperature to low and cook for 4 to 5 hours. Remove from the cooker, sprinkle with the slivered almonds and caster sugar, garnish with mint sprigs and serve with cream, ice cream or frozen yoghurt.

WASSAIL CUP

Although this cup does not contain any alcohol, it certainly feels as though it does. It is ideal to serve to those who do not drink alcohol.

SERVES	**6 to 8**	PREPARATION TIME	**5 min**	COOKING TIME	**Cook on low 2 to 3 hrs**

INGREDIENTS

600 ml (20 fl oz) clear apple juice

300 ml (10 fl oz) apple cider

300 ml (10 fl oz) black tea

2–4 tbsp raw sugar, or to taste

1 sliced lemon

5 whole cloves

1 small piece ginger, peeled and chopped

4 star anise

1 cinnamon stick, bruised

Apple slices and mint sprigs, to decorate

Preheat the cooker on high. Place all the ingredients into the cooking pot and cover with the lid. Cook on low for 2 to 3 hours, then serve in heatproof glasses, decorated with apple slices and mint sprigs.

RIGHT: *PEACH AND ALMOND CRISP*

CHOCOLATE BRIOCHE BREAD PUDDING

This dessert is real comfort food – the biggest problem is that it is so delicious you have to keep going back for more.

SERVES **4 to 6**   PREPARATION TIME **15 min**   COOKING TIME **Cook on high 3 to 4 hrs**

INGREDIENTS

2 tbsp butter

3 individual brioches or ½ large brioche

100 g (3 ½ oz) chopped stoned dates

2 tbsp brown sugar, or to taste

4 squares (100 g/ 3 ½ oz) plain chocolate, melted

3 large eggs

300 ml (10 fl oz) no-fat milk

1–2 tsp icing sugar, sieved

Cream, to serve

Preheat the slow cooker on high for 20 minutes. Lightly smear the inside of a 1.2-litre (2-pint) heatproof dish with a little of the butter. Slice the brioches and spread with the softened butter. Arrange in the buttered dish, scatter over the dates and sugar to taste. Stir the chocolate until smooth, then pour over the brioche and dates.

Beat the eggs with the milk, then pour over the brioche mixture. Place the dish in the cooker and pour hot water around it so that the water level comes half way up the dish. Cover with the lid and cook on high for 3 to 4 hours or until a skewer inserted into the centre comes out clean. Sprinkle with the icing sugar and serve with cream.

PEARS IN RUM AND MAPLE SYRUP

Select evenly shaped pears, ones that will stand upright, for this dish. Bosc pears are an ideal choice.

SERVES **4**   PREPARATION TIME **10 min**   COOKING TIME **Cook on high 3 to 5 hrs**

INGREDIENTS

4 firm pears

4 tbsp maple syrup

4 tbsp rum

300 ml (10 fl oz) water

2 strips pared orange zest

1 cinnamon stick, bruised

Cream and biscuits, to serve

Extra orange zest and cinnamon stick, to decorate

Preheat the slow cooker on high. Peel the pears, keeping them whole and, if possible, keeping the stalk intact. Place in the cooking pot. Heat the maple syrup, rum and water and bring to the boil.

Pour over the pears and add the orange zest and cinnamon stick. Cover and cook on high for 3 to 5 hours, turning the pears occasionally so they are coated in the syrup. Remove from the cooking pot and place in a serving dish. Pour the syrup into a pan, discarding the orange zest and cinnamon stick, and bring to the boil. Boil vigorously for 8 to 10 minutes until reduced slightly. Pour over the pears and serve with cream and biscuits and decorated with extra orange zest and cinnamon sticks.

LEFT: *CHOCOLATE BRIOCHE BREAD PUDDING*

SUNSET APPLES

It is important to use firm apples. You need a variety that do not break down and become fluffy during cooking; otherwise, you will find that the apples will collapse during the long cooking.

SERVES 4	PREPARATION TIME 10 min	COOKING TIME Cook on high 2 to 3 hrs

INGREDIENTS

1 to 2 tbsp butter

4 large evenly shaped firm apples such as Rome Beauty

25 g (1 oz) dried cranberries

25 g (1 oz) hazelnuts, chopped

3 tbsp brown sugar

3 tbsp raspberry jam

4 fresh bay leaves, to garnish

Cream, to serve

Preheat the cooker on high. Lightly smear the cooking pot with a little of the butter. Core the apples and rinse. Mix together the cranberries, hazelnuts and sugar and use this mixture to fill the centre of each apple. Place in the cooking pot and dot with the remaining butter.

Heat the jam with 3 tablespoons of water, stir until smooth, then pour over the apples. Cover and cook on low for 2 to 4 hours. Serve garnished with the bay leaves and with cream.

MAPLE SYRUP DESSERT

When cooking a cake-style dessert in the slow cooker, it is important that the cooker is preheated on high for 20 minutes and the dessert is cooked on high for the recommended time.

SERVES 6	PREPARATION TIME 10 min	COOKING TIME Cook on high 5 to 7 hrs

INGREDIENTS

1 tsp butter

6 tbsp maple syrup

100 g (3 ½ oz) softened butter or margarine

100 g (3 ½ oz) caster sugar

2 large eggs

½ tsp vanilla extract

100 g (3 ½ oz) self-raising flour; If substituting with plain flour, add 1 ¼ tsp baking powder and ¼ tsp salt

25 g (1 oz) ground almonds

Cream, to serve

Preheat the slow cooker on high for 20 minutes. Lightly grease a 900-ml (1 ½-pint) pudding mould with the butter and line the base with a small circle of waxed paper. Pour 4 tablespoons of the syrup in the base of the mould and reserve.

Place all the ingredients except the remaining syrup into a mixing bowl and beat until combined, then spoon into the mould and level the top. Cover loosely with a double sheet of aluminium foil. Place in the cooking pot of the slow cooker and pour around sufficient water to come halfway up the side of the mould. Cover with the lid and cook on high for 5 to 7 hours. Turn out onto a serving plate and discard the waxed paper circle. Heat the remaining syrup and pour over the cake, then serve with the cream.

RIGHT: *SUNSET APPLES*

CHOCOLATE AND ORANGE DESSERT

You can vary the flavours in this wicked dessert – try adding some ground cinnamon or ground cardamom – then you could also add some chocolate chips, dried cherries or even some raisins.

SERVES **6**   PREPARATION TIME **15 min**   COOKING TIME **Cook on high 25to 7 hrs**

INGREDIENTS

100 g (3 ½ oz) plain chocolate

100 g (3 ½ oz) margarine or butter, softened

100 g (3 ½ oz) brown sugar

2 tbsp grated orange zest

2 large eggs, beaten

100 g (3 ½ oz) self-raising flour; If substituting with plain flour, add 1 ¼ tsp baking powder and ¼ tsp salt

25 g (1 oz) ground almonds

2 tbsp unsweetened cocoa powder, sieved

1–2 tbsp orange juice

2 tsp icing sugar

Chocolate or orange sauce, or cream and fresh redcurrants or orange segments, to serve

Preheat the slow cooker on high for 20 minutes. Take a 900-ml (1 ½-pint) heatproof pudding mould, lightly butter and line the base with a small circle of waxed paper. Break the chocolate into small pieces and place over a pan of gently simmering water and heat, stirring occasionally until the chocolate has melted. Stir until smooth, reserve.

Cream the margarine or butter with the sugar and orange zest until light and fluffy, then gradually beat in the eggs, adding a little flour after each addition. When all the eggs have been added, stir in the melted chocolate followed by the remaining flour, ground almonds and cocoa powder. Mix with the orange juice to give a smooth dropping consistency. Spoon into the prepared mould and level the top. Cover loosely with a double sheet of aluminium foil.

Place in the cooking pot of the slow cooker and pour around sufficient water to come halfway up the side of the mould. Cover with the lid and cook on high for 5 to 7 hours. Turn out, discard the waxed circle and serve, dusted with icing sugar, along with chocolate or orange sauce, or with cream and fresh redcurrants or orange segments.

CREAMY RICE PUDDING

Remember to thoroughly rinse the rice before using, especially if using short-grain rice; otherwise, the pudding will be a little starchy.

SERVES **4**   PREPARATION TIME **5 min**   COOKING TIME **Cook on high 3 to 4 hrs**   AUTO COOK **4 to 7 hrs**

INGREDIENTS

1 tsp butter

50 g (1 ¾ oz) short-grain rice

2 tbsp caster sugar

150 ml (5 fl oz) evaporated milk

900 ml (30 fl oz) semi-skimmed milk

2 tsp grated orange zest

Jam or marmalade, to serve

Preheat the slow cooker on high; grease the cooking pot with the butter. Rinse the rice and place in the cooking pot. Add all the remaining ingredients (except the accompaniments) and stir well. Cover and cook on high for 3 to 4 hours. Stir, then serve with a dollop of either jam or marmalade.

LEFT: *Orange and Chocolate Dessert*

LEMON CURD

This curd is so versatile, you can make little lemon tarts, a meringue pie or serve it on scones or over ice cream for dessert.

SERVES **5 jars**   PREPARATION TIME **30 min**   COOKING TIME **Cook on low 2 to 3 hrs**

INGREDIENTS

Grated zest and juice from 8 lemons

350 g (12 oz) sugar

175 g (6 oz) unsalted butter, diced

3 large eggs

2 large egg yolks

In a medium saucepan, over low heat, heat the lemon juice, lemon zest, sugar and butter together until the sugar has dissolved and the butter has melted, stirring occasionally.

In a medium bowl, beat the eggs and egg yolks together and strain them into the lemon juice, mixing until blended.

Pour into a baking dish that will fit into your slow cooker, and cover with aluminium foil. Tie on foil with string, making a handle to easily lift the bowl, and place into the slow cooker.

Pour in hot water to come halfway up the side of the dish, cover and cook on low for 2–3 hours. Stir once or twice during cooking, if possible.

Sterilise 5 jars, pour in the curd and seal. Cover, label, and refrigerate for up to 4 weeks.

AUTUMN RELISH

Unlike other relishes, this one does not need to mature but can be used immediately. This is because of the long slow cooking.

MAKES 1.25 kg (2 ½ lb)   **PREPARATION TIME** 15 min   **COOKING TIME** Cook on high 6 to 8 hrs

INGREDIENTS

675 g (1 ½ lb) sour apples, such as Granny Smith, peeled, cored and chopped

2 large onions, peeled and chopped

1–2 red serrano chiles, seeded and chopped

225 g (8 oz) firm but ripe pears, peeled, cored and chopped

1 red pepper, seeded and chopped

2–4 garlic cloves, peeled and minced

450 g (1 lb) brown sugar

225 g (8 oz) dried apricots, chopped

1 tsp ground ginger

1 tsp ground allspice

150 ml (5 fl oz) white wine vinegar

Fresh herb sprigs, to garnish, optional

Preheat the cooker on high. Place all the ingredients in the cooking pot or large pan and heat, stirring, until the sugar has dissolved. (If using a pan, transfer to the cooking pot.) Cover and cook for 6 to 8 hours, stirring occasionally. (Do ensure that you replace the lid firmly so that the liquid does not evaporate.) Stir well, then spoon into sterilised warm, glass jars and cover with paraffin. Once cold, cover with cling film or plastic screw-top lids. Use within 3 months. Garnish with fresh herb sprigs if desired.

STICKY DATE AND TOFFEE BAKE

This pudding is for those with a serious sweet tooth. It is absolutely delicious, with a really rich, sticky base under the light fluffy cake.

SERVES 6   **PREPARATION TIME** 15 min   **COOKING TIME** Cook on high 5 to 7 hrs

INGREDIENTS

175 g (6 oz) unsalted butter, softened

175 g (6 oz) light raw sugar

2 large eggs, beaten

100 g (3 ½ oz) self-raising flour; If substituting with plain flour, add 1 ¼ tsp baking powder and ¼ tsp salt

75 g (2 ½ oz) chopped stoned dates

1 square (25 g/1 oz) plain chocolate, melted

2 tsp icing sugar, sieved

Cream or vanilla ice cream, to serve

Preheat the cooker on high. Lightly butter a 1.2-litre (2-pint) heatproof dish that will fit in the cooking pot. Beat together the butter and sugar until light and creamy, then place 3 tablespoons of the mixture in the dish and spread over the whole base. Beat the eggs gradually into the remaining butter and sugar mixture, adding a little flour after each addition. When all the eggs have been added, sieve together the remaining flour, then stir in the dates and melted chocolate. Spoon into the dish and cover with a sheet of aluminium foil.

Place in the cooker and pour sufficient hot water around to come halfway up the sides of the dish. Cover and cook on high for 5 hours. When ready to serve, place all the sauce ingredients in a pan and heat gently until blended. Serve the bake sprinkled with the icing sugar and with either cream or ice cream.

LEFT: *AUTUMN RELISH*

MULLED RED WINE

Mulled red wine is great to serve at a party, especially one in the winter. When the wine is ready, leave it in the slow cooker so it will stay warm for your guests as they come in from the cold. There is no point in splashing out on great wine and brandy, as the sugar and spices will alter its flavour, opt for cheaper brands and save yourself the difference!

SERVES **8 to 10**   PREPARATION TIME **5 min**   COOKING TIME **Cook on low 3 to 4 hrs**

INGREDIENTS

2 bottles red wine

120 ml (20 fl oz) brandy

225 g (8 oz) light brown sugar

1 orange

8 cloves

1 cinnamon stick, broken into 3 pieces

Pour the wine and brandy into the slow cooker, add the sugar and stir.

Cut the orange into 8 segments and stud each segment with a clove. Add to the slow cooker with the cinnamon stick.

Cook on low for 3 to 4 hours. Serve in heatproof glasses.

PLUM PUDDING

Some might wish to keep this very rich pudding for special occasions, such as christmas or thanksgiving, but that would be a pity. It is so good, why not serve it on a regular basis?

SERVES **8**   PREPARATION TIME **15 min**   COOKING TIME **Cook on high 8 to 12 hrs**

INGREDIENTS

100 g (3 ½ oz) unsalted butter, softened

100 g (3 ½ oz) dark raw sugar

1 tbsp grated orange zest

1 tbsp treacle

2 extra large eggs, beaten

50 g (1 ¾ oz) whole-wheat self-raising flour; If substituting with plain flour, add 1 ¼ tsp baking powder and ¼ tsp salt

175 g (6 oz) raisins

175 g (6 oz) sultanas

55 g (2 oz) dried cranberries or ready-to-eat apricots, chopped

75 g (2 ½ oz) glacé cherries, chopped

1 tsp ground mixed spice

½ tsp ground ginger

100 g (3 ½ oz) soft whole-wheat bread crumbs

2–3 tbsp brandy, sherry or orange juice

Brandy butter or cream, to serve

Lightly oil and line the base of a 1.2-litre (2-pint) pudding mould with a small circle of waxed paper and set aside. Beat together the butter, sugar and orange zest until light and fluffy, then stir in the treacle. Gradually add the eggs, a little at a time, beating well and adding a spoonful of flour after each addition.

When all the eggs have been added, stir in any remaining flour and the rest of the ingredients except for the brandy, sherry or fruit juice. Mix well, then add sufficient brandy, sherry or juice to give a soft dropping consistency. Spoon into the prepared mould and cover with a sheet of waxed paper and double sheet of aluminium foil folded with a pleat in the centre to allow for expansion. Place on a sling of foil for ease of lifting.

Place in the cooking pot of the cooker and pour around sufficient hot water to come three-quarters of the way up the mould. Cover with the lid and cook on high for 8 to 12 hours, adding water as necessary. Remove and either serve immediately with brandy butter or cream or recover and store in a cool dry place until required. (Reheat in the cooker with water poured around as before for at least 4 hours.)

RIGHT: *MULLED RED WINE*

GLACÉ CHERRY AND GINGER BREAD AND BUTTER PUDDING

You can use fruited bread, or ordinary white or brown bread for this recipe. Try it with sliced brioche, or even a seeded loaf. Whichever you use, you will be delighted with the finished dish.

SERVES 4 **PREPARATION TIME** 15 min **COOKING TIME** Cook on high 3 to 4 hrs

INGREDIENTS

2 tbsp butter, softened

6–8 slices fruit loaf

50 g (1 ¾ oz) glacé cherries, chopped

50 g (1 ¾ oz) crystallised or preserved ginger, chopped

50 g (1 ¾ oz) dried blueberries or cranberries

1 tbsp grated orange zest

1 tsp ground ginger

2 tbsp maple syrup

2 extra large eggs

240 ml (8 fl oz) single cream

Caster sugar, for sprinkling

Cream or custard, to serve

Preheat the cooker on high. Lightly butter a 1.2-litre (2-pint) ovenproof dish that will sit in your cooking pot and set aside. Spread the bread with the remaining butter and cut into small triangles. Arrange half of the bread in the base of the dish and sprinkle with the cherries, ginger, blueberries or cranberries and finally the grated orange zest. Top with the remaining buttered bread.

Blend the ginger and maple syrup together, then beat in the eggs followed by the cream. Pour over the bread and leave to stand for 30 minutes. Place in the cooking pot, using an aluminium foil sling for ease of lifting. Pour sufficient hot water to come halfway up the sides of the dish. Cover and cook on high for 3 to 5 hours or until the custard has set. Sprinkle with sugar and serve with cream or custard.

SPICY WINTER COMPÔTE

Fruit, whether fresh or dried, cooked in the slow cooker retains all its natural flavours; the spices, wine or juices used in the cooking slowly blend into the fruit.

SERVES 6 to 8 **PREPARATION TIME** 5 min **COOKING TIME** Cook on low 7 to 8 hrs

INGREDIENTS

450 g (1 lb) mixed dried fruit

100 g (3 ½ oz) raisins

2–4 tbsp brown sugar

4 whole cloves

½ tsp ground mixed spice

¼ tsp freshly grated nutmeg

1 cinnamon stick, bruised

2 strips thinly pared lemon zest

240 ml (8 fl oz) white wine

300 ml (10 fl oz) orange juice

Mascarpone cheese or plain yoghurt, to serve

Preheat the slow cooker on high. Rinse the mixed dried fruits and place in the cooking pot with the raisins; sprinkle in the sugar, the spices and the lemon zest. If you have a sweet tooth, increase the sugar up to 4 tablespoons. Pour over the white wine and orange juice, then cover and cook on low for 7 to 8 hours before serving with either mascarpone cheese or yoghurt.

RIGHT: GLACÉ CHERRY AND GINGER BREAD AND BUTTER PUDDING

CRÈME BRÛLÉE

If desired, you can put some fresh fruits in the base of the dish before pouring in the custard. Use fruits that are fairly firm in texture; otherwise, they may collapse too much during the long cooking.

SERVES **4** PREPARATION TIME **15 min** COOKING TIME **Cook on high 3 to 6 hrs**

INGREDIENTS

3 large eggs

175 g (6 oz) caster sugar

1 tsp vanilla extract

240 ml (8 fl oz) single cream

120 ml (4 fl oz) double cream

120 ml (4 fl oz) whole milk

Preheat the cooker on high. Beat the eggs with 3 tablespoons of the sugar and the vanilla extract until thoroughly blended. Slightly warm the cream and milk, then beat into the egg mixture. Strain into 4 to 6 individual ramekin dishes, ensuring that they fit inside the cooking pot, then place in the pot.

Pour around sufficient hot water to come three-quarters of the way up the sides of the dishes. Cover and cook on low for 3 hours or until set. Remove and allow to cool.

Sprinkle the tops with the remaining caster sugar. Place under a preheated grill and cook until the sugar melts and caramelises. You will need to turn the dishes to ensure that the sugar melts evenly. Remove from the grill, cool, then chill until required.

APPLE AND CRANBERRY PUDDING

Any dried fruit, such as chopped apricots, prunes, mango, papaya, cherries or a mixture of fruits, can be used in place of the cranberries in this dessert.

SERVES **6** PREPARATION TIME **15 min** COOKING TIME **Cook on high 4 to 6 hrs**

INGREDIENTS

120 ml (4 fl oz) sunflower oil

175 g (6 oz) brown sugar

2 large eggs

1 tbsp grated orange zest

175 g (6 oz) self-raising whole-wheat flour; If substituting with plain flour, add 1 ¼ tsp baking powder and ¼ tsp salt

1 tsp ground cinnamon

75 g (2 ½ oz) dried cranberries

1 sour apple, such as Granny Smith, peeled, cored and chopped

1–2 tbsp orange juice

Cream, to serve

Preheat the slow cooker on high for 20 minutes. Lightly oil a 900-ml (1 ½-pint) pudding mould and place a small round of waxed paper in the base. Beat the sugar, oil and eggs together; then add the orange zest, flour and cinnamon. Beat well, then stir in the cranberries and apple with sufficient orange juice to give a dropping consistency. Spoon into the prepared mould and cover with a double sheet of aluminium foil. Place in the slow cooker cooking pot. Cook on high for 4 to 6 hours, then turn out and serve with cream.

RIGHT: *CRÈME BRÛLÉE*

CHOCOLATE FONDUE

There is something really decadent about chocolate, so when you are in need of a chocolate fix why not go completely overboard and indulge in this rich and luscious chocolate fondue?

....

SERVES **6 to 8**   PREPARATION TIME **5 min**   COOKING TIME **Cook on low 1 to 3 hrs**

INGREDIENTS

12 squares plain chocolate

240 ml (8 fl oz) double cream

2 tbsp maple syrup, or to taste

3–4 tbsp brandy or Cointreau

Assorted fresh fruits and small sweet firm cakes for dipping

Preheat the cooker on high. Break the chocolate into pieces and place in the cooking pot with the cream, maple syrup and brandy or Cointreau. Cover and cook for 1 hour or until the chocolate has melted. Stir until smooth, then either use immediately with the fruits and cakes for dipping or keep on low for up to 2 hours.

GINGERBREAD

Although the top of this gingerbread is not crisp, the flavour and texture is superb – try it for yourself and see.

....

SERVES **10 to 12**   PREPARATION TIME **15 min**   COOKING TIME **Cook on high 6 to 8 hrs**

INGREDIENTS

175 g (6 oz) brown sugar

100 g (3 ½ oz) unsalted butter

75 g (2 ½ oz) golden syrup

75 g (2 ½ oz) treacle

2–3 tsp ground ginger

100 g (3 ½ oz) plain flour

100 g (3 ½ oz) white self-raising flour

1 ¼ tsp baking powder

Pinch salt

1 large egg

120 ml (4 fl oz) milk

½ tsp baking soda

Preheat cooker on high while preparing the ingredients. Lightly oil and base line an 18-cm (7-inch) round cake pan or a 1.25-kg (2 ¾-lb) dish. Heat the sugar, butter, golden syrup and treacle in a saucepan until melted, stirring until smooth. Sieve the ground ginger with the flours, baking powder and salt into a mixing bowl, then beat in the melted sugar mixture. Cool slightly, then beat in the egg and stir well.

Warm the milk, stir in the baking soda and stir into the mixture. Mix well, then pour into the prepared cake pan or dish and place on top of an upturned ramekin or other small, heatproof dish.

Pour around sufficient hot water to come halfway up the sides of the pan.

Cover and cook on high for 6 to 8 hours. Remove from the pan, cool slightly, then invert onto a wire cooling rack. Cut into slices to serve. Store in an airtight container.

LEFT: *CHOCOLATE FONDUE*

INDEX